"At the Heart of Leadership" is a breath of fresh air – a hands on, practical approach to becoming a better leader. Josh provides common sense techniques that I use every day to gain clear insight and improve performance. Very enjoyable and it really works: A must read for every leader."

- Jimmy Daniel, Global Leadership Institute, FedEx Express, USA

"I've worked with hundreds of leaders from around the world over the last 20 years. This experience has shown me that Emotional Intelligence can make the difference between a good and an extraordinary leader. At the Heart of Leadership shows clearly and precisely why that is true. This book is easy to read, understand and apply in everyday business, even for a non-English native speaker. It is written in a very engaging way and motivates one to learn about leadership at its best."

- Martina Mathis, Leadership Development Manager, Siemens AG Munich/Germany

"Assuming that all leaders today 'get' that relationships are the pathways to progress and ultimately success, the information assembled here by Joshua Freedman is an important read for any leader looking to take it higher. The information is clear and intriguing and the examples are relevant and interesting and applicable to all aspects of life. Thanks Joshua for your leadership and devotion to the subject of emotional intelligence."

- Arlene Pfeiff, Vice President, Technologies, American Express, USA

"Leadership is about exerting influence, nurturing relationship and willing collaboration between leaders and followers. "At the Heart of Leadership" by Joshua Freedman touches these in a powerful, simple to understand and easy to apply principles for leaders at every level even at home with your families........ It's a must read leadership book!"

- Abd Rahim Matusin, Head, Leadership and Personal Development, Brunei Shell Petroleum

"Across cultures, leading with heart is one of the oldest concepts in management, but it's all too rare in practice. In the complexity of business in China today, it's even more important than ever. However, this is the only book I know that tackles this difficult form of art by putting practical tools in the hands of business leaders. In the past six years, we have been loyally using this model to empower business leaders – and it creates measurable impact."

- Wendy Wu, CEO, New Leaders Group, China

"In many graduate management programs students are taught that professionalism means leaving your emotions out of the workplace. This book points out the costly errors of this position, while reinforcing the viewpoint that emotions actually drive people, and that people drive performance. Mr. Freedman provides us with a useful EQ framework and a rich language, enabling a more precise diagnosis of one's level of effectiveness in engaging emotionally and constructively with others. I consider this book a primary professional development companion text, providing sufficient examples and exercises to support the development of a more mature and productive workplace climate."

- Christopher L. Washington, Ph.D. - Provost and Senior Vice President, Franklin University, USA

"At the heart of Leadership is a high impact must read for all leaders. It's a practical guide that has great concepts for all leaders to adopt and key messages that really hit home! I love the moments in the book where you, as a leader can stop and pause to reflect and gain insight into your own methods and behaviours. It is so good that I often share the little nuggets of wisdom found in this book with the leaders in my organization which creates some great "AHA!" moments."

- Abi White, Director of Performance, Talent and Training, TECOM Investments, UAE

"I've worked with hundreds of leaders over the last 40 years. The few who exemplify a high emotional intelligence stand head and shoulders above others in their performance, quality of life, and the lasting value they create for all stakeholders. In At the Heart of Leadership Freedman shows why that's true – and he offers us an opportunity to grow to become the leaders we've always meant to be. Highly recommended."

- George McCown, President and CEO, McCown De Leeuw & Co, USA

"After three decades of combat service, I've seen first hand that effective leaders have a special gift to keep people together and stable under intense pressure. Real leaders have "emotional intelligence" to connect. In today's high stress and high tension environment, be at home or at the job, the situation is getting more explosive by the day: Emotional intelligence is a God sent solution.   But how do we actually develop these skills? "Heart of Leadership" fills this gap to make Emotional Intelligence a resource for the day to day life of every manager. Blessings to Josh for this beautiful work, and with gratitude to God giving the power of EQ to all of us."

- Colonel MGS Nagi, Retd, India Country Manager,
Engee Enterprises UK Ltd

"If I have to describe in one sentence what the six seconds EQ model has done for me, I would say: 'clear self-direction.' With the logical flow of the three pursuits, I'm now able to connect my true self with my long-term noble goals. I knew where I was, and where I wanted to go. Now I know the path that connects both. In addition, I now possess the knowledge to understand, not only the EQ competencies that have helped me lead teams in the past, but also the ones that I need to focus and develop right away. Last, but not least, I have a clear understanding that the engine that will keep me focused and motivated is within me."

-Gerardo Amaya, Business and Technology Consultant, Canada

"A simple and practical guide for leaders to leverage their EQ skills at the critical intersection of self-awareness and the daily challenges within the business environment. It reinforces the potential each leader has to use emotional intelligence to increase effective decision making and organizational performance. This is a must read book for leaders preparing for or in the midst of personal or organizational transformation."

- Timothy J. Gillum, Ph.D., Senior Manager Quality/Training, Baxter Healthcare, USA

"Many people in leadership positions get stuck in dealing with the people issues in their organizations. As a leader in the health care system, often what gets in the way of success are issues related to staff attitude and behavior and not the technical skills. I have found and used the skills presented in the book At the Heart of Leadership with great results both personally and with our employees. Josh has really hit the nail on the head. Every leader who desires progress and customer satisfaction should go grab this book and thoroughly digest it, and seek to empower his people with the skills of Emotional Intelligence. It is the difference maker!"

- Dr Ebong Akpabio, Health and Development Consultant, Centre for Health and Development, Namibia

"The Heart of Leadership is an outstanding and eminently practical guide for anyone who hopes to be a great mentor, to influence with integrity and to truly lead organizations. Joshua Freedman has a unique gift for engaging people from all walks of life in learning and professional transformation – this book is a must-read for leaders everywhere!"

– Annie McKee, CEO Teleos Leadership Institute; coauthor, Primal Leadership, USA

"I know, I know, when you hear the term Emotional Intelligence your face contorts into a sarcastic look and you exclaim, 'Isn't this just another touchy feely kum-bye-ya concept' then roll your eyes. I am here to tell you it is NOT.

If you are a leader that wishes to achieve results while supporting healthy growth and development of yourself and your employees, this is the book for you. *At the Heart of Leadership* provides leaders with real world practical tools and knowledge needed to create a workplace that succeeds – and more importantly, a workplace that thrives."

- Lisa Moore, Sr. Learning and Talent Management Specialist,
FedEx Services, USA

At the Heart of Leadership

How to Get Results with Emotional Intelligence

Joshua Freedman

Introduction by Peter Salovey

sixseconds
EMOTIONAL INTELLIGENCE PRESS

Copyright ©2007, 2012, Joshua Freedman
Published by Six Seconds
PO Box 1985
Freedom, CA 95019
Web: www.6seconds.org
Email: staff@6seconds.org
Phone: (831) 763-1800

Cover Design by Mark Lee, Incite Partners

Library of Congress Cataloging-in-Publication Data
Freedman, Joshua
At the Heart of Leadership: How to Get Results with Emotional Intelligence / by Joshua Freedman; Introduction by Peter Salovey.
1. Leadership. 2 Business

Printed in China
Third Edition, Revised and Updated. 2nd printing.

ISBN: 978-1-935667-16-2

www.6seconds.org/tools

Contents

Part One: Emotions Are Assets

Part Two: EQ in Action

Table of Figures

Introduction

Peter Salovey, Ph.D.

Provost and Chris Argyris
Professor of Psychology
Yale University

At The Heart of Leadership represents a new approach to factors that predict success in the workplace. It is certainly the case that employees with strong technical skills and general, analytic intelligence perform better than individuals who do not share these attributes. But sometimes very talented individuals – intelligent individuals with strong job-related skills – fail. And we can learn something from their failures because often they are due to problems with co-workers, disputes with managers, or a lack of practical intelligence, or "street smarts."

Since we published our first article on the topic in 1990,[1] we have argued that there is another kind of wisdom, called *emotional intelligence*, that might help us to understand better who succeeds and who does not in business environments. Emotional intelligence might be thought of as the ability to perceive, understand, and regulate one's moods and emotions in order to use them to succeed in life. There are several different models of emotional intelligence in the scientific literature, but all of them share a common emphasis on psychological skills and attributes not measured by traditional IQ tests nor necessarily explicitly job-related but that make a difference to one's success in personal relationships, family life, and in the workplace.

Emotional intelligence is not the ability to suppress negative emotions or encourage positive ones. Our particular model of emotional intelligence emphasizes four distinct sets of abilities, what we have sometimes called *branches*, as in the branches of a tree.[2] The first branch of emotional intelligence, *perceiving emotions*, is the ability to detect and decipher emotions in faces, pictures, voices, and artifacts. It also includes the ability to identify one's own emotions. Perceiving emotions may represent the most basic aspect of emotional intelligence, as it makes all other processing of emotional information possible.

The second branch of emotional intelligence, *using emotions*, is the ability to harness emotions to facilitate various cognitive activities, such as thinking and problem solving. For example, being in a slightly sad mood helps people conduct careful, methodical work. Conversely, a happy mood can stimulate creative and innovative thinking. The emotionally intelligent person can capitalize fully upon his or her changing moods in order to best fit the task at hand.

The third branch of emotional intelligence, *understanding emotions*, is the ability to comprehend emotion language and to appreciate complicated relationships between emotions. For example, understanding emotions encompasses the ability to be sensitive to slight variations between emotions, such as the difference between happy and ecstatic. Furthermore, it includes the ability to recognize and describe how emotions evolve over time, such as how shock can turn into grief.

The fourth branch of emotional intelligence, *managing emotions*, consists of the ability to regulate emotions in both ourselves and in others. Everyone is familiar with times in their lives when they have temporarily, and sometimes embarrassingly, lost control of their emotions. The fourth branch also includes the ability to manage the emotions of others. For example, an emotionally intelligent leader might increase her own anger and use it to deliver a powerful speech in order to inspire others. Therefore, the emotionally intelligent person can harness emotions, even negative ones, and manage them to achieve intended goals.

In some of our research, we have discovered that individuals who have these skills perform better at work.[3] For example, employees of a North American health insurance company, who worked in teams each headed by a supervisor, completed measures of their emotional intelligence. Later, these employees were asked to rate each other on the qualities they displayed at work, such as handling stress and conflict well and displaying leadership potential. Supervisors were also asked to rate their employees. Employees with higher emotional intelligence were rated by their colleagues as easier to deal with and more responsible for creating a positive work environment. Their supervisors rated them as more interpersonally sensitive, more tolerant of stress, more sociable, and having greater potential for leadership. Moreover, greater emotional intelligence was related to higher salary and moving up in the company.[4]

There are many pressures on leaders today that make emotional intelligence particularly important. One is the need to work with people from all over the globe. For example, the Chinese economy is undergoing a rapid transformation and one that has increasingly internationalized the workforces of its companies and the global reach of its products and services. Internationalized workforces and business settings can lead to misunderstandings due to cultural differences, and some of these cultural differences have to do with emotions. The emotionally intelligent American, for instance, knows that when doing business in China it is important to develop a trusting relationship with a potential customer before making a business proposal. But I have also observed emotional misunderstandings get in the way of good business on many occasions.

It may be helpful to recognize that Europeans and Americans derive their business style in part from a different cultural tradition than do East Asians. Europeans and Americans have long admired the Ancient Greeks, such as Aristotle and Plato, with their emphasis on individual uniqueness and personal agency (individual control over future events). Chinese tradition has emphasized harmony (rather than agency) and self-control so as to have good relations with other people. Confucius wrote of the importance of controlling one's emotions in order to foster more harmonious interactions with other people, especially within the family. Not surprisingly, Europeans and Americans are more likely to believe that there is a "right answer" to a problem that can be arrived at through logic. Chinese people may be more likely to embrace the idea that there is truth on both sides of a debate and that the solution to a dispute might be in a third or middle way.[5]

The important thing to note is that these different intellectual and cultural traditions lead to differences in emotional styles that then have consequences for the way business is conducted. For instance, North Americans are more likely to arrive a little late to a meeting (or even later to a social event), while Chinese business people are more likely to arrive right on time or early, whether it is a formal meeting or a social occasion. The emotional consequence of this difference in practice is that North Americans and Chinese will have different emotional reactions to the timeliness of their business partners. Chinese managers may be shocked and insulted by an American who arrives a few minutes late, for example. An American may be shocked by the very many gifts he or she is given by Chinese business partners and may be embarrassed not to have remembered to bring gifts of his own to distribute. These are just some obvious examples of business practices that differ in East Asia versus North America, but they may reflect deeper philosophical differences that have emotional consequences.

The study of emotions in the workplace and the development of emotional intelligence are important for reasons that transcend the growing internationalization of businesses and the potential for culturally-based misunderstandings. Emotions have been critical in our survival as individuals and as a species. The world that we live in is exceedingly complex, and accessing our emotions is important to behaving adaptively. Emotions motivate our behavior and focus our thinking in ways that are helpful to us. Emotions are not superfluous. They do not merely add interest to our lives; they are critical to our very survival. Almost every theory of emotions suggests that emotions convey important information about the environment that helps us to thrive and survive.

It is an honor for me to introduce this book to you. It was written by Joshua Freedman, whom I have known and admired for many years, and published by a wonderful organization very concerned about bringing an understanding of emotions to the workplace. This book is especially powerful because it brings together the perspective of a teacher, emphasizing the development of social and emotional skills, and a leader with a great deal of experience running and working with organizations. This union of education and organizational behavior has motivated an experiential approach to learning about emotional intelligence for the workplace. The skills that represent emotional intelligence can be learned by studying vivid case examples and practicing the skills themselves. And that is the approach of *At The Heart of Leadership*.

Peter Salovey
New Haven, Connecticut

Notes from the Introduction

1   Salovey, P., & Mayer, J.D. (1990). "Emotional Intelligence." *Imagination, Cognition, and Personality*, 9, 185–211.

2   Mayer, J.D., & Salovey, P. (1997). What is Emotional Intelligence? In P. Salovey & D. Sluyter (Eds.), *Emotional Development and Emotional Intelligence: Educational Implications* (pp. 3–31). New York: Basic Books.

3   Lopes, P.N., Grewal, D., Kadis, J., Gall, M., & Salovey, P. (2006). "Evidence that Emotional Intelligence is Related to Job Performance and Affect and Attitudes at Work." *Psicothema*, 18, 132-138.

4   Caruso, D. R., & Salovey, P. (2004). *The Emotionally Intelligent Manager.* San Francisco, CA: Jossey-Bass.

5   Nisbett, R.E. (2003). *The Geography of Thought: How Asians and Westerners Think Differently . . . and Why.* New York: The Free Press.

Preface to the Third Edition

In 1992, serendipity led me to join the faculty of a remarkable school where emotional and academic development were considered interwoven threads for success. It was a magical place where learning was vibrant and joyful and serious and deep. Karen McCown launched the school in 1967 to be a model for the revolutionary idea that emotional and academic development could be integrated. In around 1983 Dr. Anabel Jensen became the Executive Director there, and together they refined Karen's concept and won two Federal Blue Ribbons for Excellence in Education. In 1993, author Daniel Goleman visited and witnessed **Self-Science**, a process for teaching children and adults about emotions and decisions. He told us about the work of Peter Salovey and others who called this "emotional intelligence." In his 1995 book, Goleman wrote about the Self-Science program as a model for teaching EQ – and when that became an international best-seller, many people called us saying, "The skills of EQ are exactly what we need - and Goleman says you know how to teach us: Can you show us how?"

In 1997, Karen and Anabel invited me to join them in an adventure to answer this request. Together with our colleague Marsha Rideout, we launched Six Seconds to teach this practical, proven approach to teaching EQ. A year later we offered our first certification program to show others how to use these methods, and we received a shocking gift.

Given our backgrounds, we'd expected that most of the people interested in how to teach EQ would be from elementary and secondary education... and we imagined they'd be primarily from the local area. We were wrong. Our first EQ Certification participants were managers and leaders, nurses and counselors, professors and HR directors, as well as teachers and parents... and they flew from Johannesburg and London, Singapore and Beijing, Caracas and Toronto, and many points between. From them, and literally thousands more professionals over the next decade, we learned how to make emotional intelligence both transformational and practical.

Over the years, occasionally people would come to these courses and say: "I want to bring this work to Singapore.... Mexico... South Africa.... the UK... the Middle East..." Others would say, "This is the work I've been looking for all my life: I don't need you to pay me, but I want to work for you." At first, we didn't know what either of these really meant, nor how to utilize the gifts of alliance that kept coming forward. Together we've learned, and built a remarkable organization.

Now we are led by change makers in 11 countries. We are a powerful network of emotional intelligence experts (and compared to others doing this work, by far the largest in reach and experience). At this point we've published dozens of world-class development programs, books, assessments, and learning tools. We run seven different certification programs each year in four global regions. Perhaps most importantly, we've identified why we do this work together - why this is vital today:

All around the globe there are people committed to creating positive change. Perhaps you are one of these leaders – perhaps you look at your team, your organization, your family, your schools, your community, our world, and say: We can do and be more. We can be sustainable and prosperous. We can be competitive and compassionate. It's time to step up, not just 2% or 5%, but to a whole new level of what it means to perform. We call this "Positive Change," and our mission is to support people like you to be more powerful in this shift toward a flourishing future. To be leaders worth following.

There are many many people whose insights have made this work thrive, and whose ideas are central to this book. While my name is on the cover, the truth is that this book is a compilation of what I've learned from colleague and clients as I've been privileged to spend the last 15 years working full-time on teaching and learning about emotions. Thank you for being an integral part of this adventure.

In addition to those already mentioned, I want to specifically thank the Managing Directors of our international offices who lead Six Seconds: Massimiliano Ghini, Jayne Morrison, Granville D'Souza, Wendy Wu, Melissa Donaldson, Veruska Genarri, Nadeem Nahas, Dexter Valles, FC Law, Yasuhiro Tanabe, and Anthony Dio-Martin.

Finally, I'd like to say that I wish I was fully successful at practicing the skills we teach. I know I'm not... and I'm working on getting better. No one knows that quite as well as my wife and children. As I wrote in the First Edition:

To my most important teachers and inspirations to keep learning – Emma, Max, and Patty – thank you for your patience as I tilt at these windmills.

Joshua Freedman
Freedom, California 2012

About the Author

Chief Executive Officer of Six Seconds, Joshua Freedman is a catalyst for positive change. A founder of the world's most extensive emotional intelligence organization, he leads a network of professionals assisting individuals and organizations to create sustainable success by increasing wisdom, compassion, and insight.

Joshua is one of a handful of experts in the world with over a decade of full-time, proven experience in emotional intelligence development. Joshua and the Six Seconds' team deliver transformational programs and consult with a wide range of organizations around the globe to strengthen leadership, accelerate change, and build organizations where talent thrives. From teaching change leaders in the US Navy, to deepening people-leadership at FedEx, to building a customer-oriented culture at Rotana, to reinvigorating learning for lifelong success at Singapore Polytechnic, Six Seconds' consultants are people-experts blending hard science and business acumen to fuel positive change.

Freedman is the author of INSIDE CHANGE and coauthor of THE VITAL ORGANIZATION. He also authored seven validated psychometric assessments (including the SEI Brain Brief and Organizational Vital Signs), as well as numerous development programs, learning tools, and training modules, he is one of the most prolific contributors to making the science of emotional intelligence practical and transformational.

Freedman co-developed Six Seconds' EQ Certification Training which he has delivered on five continents as master-trainer to thousands of professionals seeking practical tools for learning and teaching emotional intelligence.

Joshua's applied research focuses on organizational climate and the factors that enhance individual and team performance. He has worked with a range of organizations to identify key relationship and emotional intelligence factors that limit and enhance success, and then to fuel people-leadership to drive positive change.

Joshua champions emotional intelligence development around the world. He has helped launch emotional intelligence initiatives and organizations in nearly two dozen countries. He instigated the first global virtual conference on emotions and leadership, 24EQ, free to thousands of participants worldwide. He chairs the International NexusEQ Conferences, the premier forum for the unique intersection of science, learning, and leadership.

Living in a small town on the central coast of California with his wife and children, Joshua enjoys walking on the beach and gardening. He graduated *Magna Cum Laude* from the World Arts and Cultures program at UCLA.

Part One:

Emotions Are Assets

Chapter One

Bad Feelings?

A true story: "Carl" is an executive director running a complex service business in three US states.[1] He should be a star: He is smart, energetic, self-controlled, and has extensive knowledge about the business. Passionately committed to this company's work, Carl works incredibly hard and he has many strong people-skills. Infallibly positive, he always says, "yes," even to requests that seem impossible.

The VP, Alex, is a powerful, dynamic business person and an incredibly energetic leader — a very forceful person. Alex comes from another part of the business, and despite his skills, he doesn't actually have a lot of depth of experience in the part of the business Carl runs. Carl and Alex could be a dream team. But there is a tragic flaw.

The business is in some trouble — not irreparable, but very challenging (the Chairman later tells me it's one of the worst business challenges he's ever seen). But Carl needs to show he can handle it. Often in private conversation, Carl confesses to me he feels frustrated and anxious about the business challenges and he doesn't think he's got Alex's support. Instead of dealing with this fear, Alex does "the normal thing" and refocuses on the tasks at hand. He values being "in charge" so he pushes these worrisome feelings aside.

Carl's decision to ignore his feelings of frustration and fear cause him to take on too much, too fast. Because he is uncomfortable with "bad feelings," and the lack of trust between him and Alex, Carl often speaks as if the business situation is better than the reality. At the months go by, the business is actually getting better – but the relationship between the leaders is falling apart.

Alex picks up this mismatch between Carl's words and his heart. Eventually, he privately starts to call Carl "Mr. Teflon" because Carl's reports always minimize any problems, the issues just didn't seem to stick.

Alex is also to blame for the poor partnership. Long before the issue came to a head, he could have had an honest conversation with Carl and opened the door for real dialogue. He sensed Carl's distress but he was impatient with it. He did not want to have a confrontation (because he did not like dealing with the fallout) and so the situation escalated.

Ultimately the VP reaches a tipping point of mistrust, and Carl is fired. The company loses a real asset in Carl and about six months of progress. Carl loses a job that was ideal for him. Not because these leaders lacked business skills or product knowledge, and certainly not because of poor self control – rather the opposite: because they pushed aside "bad feelings."

In my work teaching leaders around the world, I've met dozens of people like Carl and Alex in similar situations. In every country (I've trained people from over 50), of all ages and pursuits, I see this dynamic at play.

I also see the other extreme: there are people who wallow in self-pity or vent their rage – obviously this is at least as destructive.

Is there is a middle ground where people are real without being hurtful, face the problems without painting everything awful, and access the power and wisdom of emotions? That's what it means to be emotionally intelligent – and this book will help you understand that vision, see the business benefits, and begin to apply this new way of leading.

Most people come to me thinking emotional intelligence will help them control negative emotions. My hope is that emotional intelligence will help you see that there is no such thing; instead you'll find it something much better. With "real EQ," you'll be able to consider that emotions are assets, and if you manage them intelligently you will gain incredible value in your work – and in your life. When you shift to this belief, you will stop fighting with yourself and develop real self-efficacy. You will do your best more often, make better decisions, and engage the full commitment and energy of those you lead.

This book will show you how to use a simple process that you can engage to build competitive advantage, like a propeller driving a ship, a force to move you forward. As you do so, you'll also gain tremendous corollary benefits in your work and personal relationships, your health, and your satisfaction, even joy, as you lead your life.

Feelings at Work?

I was recently training a group of Chaplains who are officers in the US Marine Corps. One Lieutenant said, "I'm not about to tell a Marine Sergeant, 'Before you storm the hill, stop and ask your squad how they're feeling.'" Yet every successful (i.e., living) Sergeant knows exactly how his team members feel. Perhaps more than any other organization, the Marines are keenly aware of the power of emotion. **They just don't call it that.** They talk about "having your head in the right place," and "oorah," and they even use the word "courage," but it's a tough thing, not something "sissy" like a feeling.

This is true in most organizations where my team and I consult. While feelings are everywhere and every person is constantly aware, at some level, of their own and others' emotions, they perceive that feelings are not a subject of daily conversation. Yet most leaders acknowledge "trust," "loyalty," and "commitment" (which all come from emotion) are critical ingredients inside the organization, and certainly with customers. I suspect that no matter where you work, you'll find people talk about feelings in some special "corporate code."

When I was a teen I has the opportunity to intern with a

film company making high-end TV commercials. The crew were a bunch of highly skilled, highly paid professionals at the top of their game, and communication was constant and essential – at that time it cost a client about $200 per second that the cameras were rolling, and an average shoot involved some 20 hours of film that would be edited into a 30-second commercial. I still remember some of the "code words" they used. "I'm not trying to get in your rice bowl" meant "please don't be defensive." "Flag on the play" meant "Don't be hurtful." And when a producer told me, "I'll have you picking up cigarette butts from here 'till Tuesday" it meant he was offended by the punk kid who asked too many questions (that would be me).

From "the investors are jittery" to "my gut tells me" to "it's time to get back in the game," emotions are very much a part of corporate culture. If you watch and listen you will begin to see and hear emotions everywhere.

So while I'm not telling the Marine Sergeant to have group therapy before storming the hill, I am suggesting that he pay close attention to these powerful and basic tools for understanding and interacting with his unit. It's something he's already keenly aware of, it's just not something he usually talks about in this direct way. The Marines know something vital about leadership; they don't use the "feeling" words, but it shows in their organizational culture – and it's the basic message of our work:

**Emotions drive people,
and people drive performance.**

So how do you tap into those powerful forces? It starts by recognizing emotions are assets, assets you can manage to gain the competitive advantage you need to thrive in a challenging world. As you leverage those assets, you build "emotional capital," an essential component of a high performing organization. An asset that creates breakthrough performance, now, and into the future.

I'll Never Say That to My Children

I have a vivid memory of storming down the long hallway of my father's house on the way to slam my bedroom door, swearing vehemently that if I ever had children, I would never say, "Because I told you so!"

Yet several years ago, I found myself saying those very words to my son. In my exasperation (desperation sometimes) to get him to do as I asked, I was "in reaction" and playing back the messages I'd heard as a child.

We all do that. When we're stuck, under pressure, hurt, or angry, it's easy to slip into unconscious patterns of reaction. When we don't know what else to say, we repeat what we've seen and heard.

So how many times in your life did you hear messages that you should suppress your emotions? When you were excited you were told, "be quiet," "sit still," "mind your manners." When you were sad you were told, "big boys / girls don't cry." When angry, "Be polite! If you have nothing nice to say, don't say anything at all." These messages are pervasive all over the world. So we grow up learning one big lesson about emotions: They are bad.

So, for several thousand years at least,[2] mankind has attempted to form societies, businesses, and families based on logic. We've made war on feelings, belittled those who show any emotion but anger, intimidated those who express them as weak and worthless, and dismissed them as "womanish" and irrational.

One only has to read the headlines to see how well that system is working. Global economic collapse. Unprecedented polarization of political "discourse." Inconceivable environmental depredation. **The old way of thinking is not working.**

And nowhere is this mindset more pervasive than the corporate culture.

I believe that dismissing and diminishing emotions has led to global terrorism (suicide bombers who are deculturated until they feel nothing), to rampant business corruption (Wall Street executives who dismiss the warning signs of their own discomfort), to irreparable environmental depredations (oil execs who push aside their own doubts to allow inadequate protection on deepwater wells), and unprecedented levels of depression, obesity, divorce, and consumption. People cut off from feelings are making poor decisions.

To continue on this path is pure folly. We have the evidence of our own senses coupled with extensive scientific proof

*You may never know what results
come of your action,*

*but if you do nothing
there will be no result.*

Mahatma Gandhi

that emotions are real, essential, and valuable.[3] In Six Seconds' programs around the world I hear people say that their lives are forever changed by gaining access to the wisdom of their own feelings.

Before my eyes I've seen people change the direction of their lives, wake up, find love and purpose and hope. I've seen what happens when they tap into that inner volcano that we can all access as a deep source of human power and potential, and truly lead. It's surprising and challenging and unbelievably easy – because emotional intelligence is your birthright. Every one of us is born with this incredible gift of inner wisdom and power. Now you have an opportunity to open that gift again, strengthen it, and gain a world of benefit.

Choosing to Lead

You have a choice to make.

It's a choice about how to live and lead – a choice each of us makes many many times every day. It's a choice between living on autopilot and living on purpose.

Each moment, each interaction, gives us the chance to choose, again and again, deciding if we will let our unconscious patterns drive us, or if we'll make conscious choices to carefully do our very best.

If everything in your life is going the way you want it to, there really is no need for you to read this book, nor to learn about emotional intelligence. You're successful, you're happy, your relationships are great, and you sleep well at night – you probably already know all you need to about emotional intelligence!

If, on the other hand, there are any aspects of your work and life that you'd like to improve, especially in the way you relate to yourself and others, emotional intelligence will provide insights and tools that may help.

Many leaders I know regret the way they spend their days. They say, "That wasn't the real me," or "Today I was not the kind of leader I really mean to be."

How about you? Are you going to bed every night saying, "YES - I did my *very best* today!" Are you waking up each morning hungry for the day to start so you can contribute a little more to the quality of the world? It is my experience, in research, in working with leaders, and in my own leadership and life, that emotional intelligence helps create that kind fulfillment.

Emotional intelligence is not a "silver bullet," it will not fix all your problems and it is not all there is to great leadership. Great leadership requires excellence in many areas – strategy, execution, discipline, innovation, analysis. Being smart about feelings may not even be the most important one of these, but it certainly is the one that's gotten the least attention and so causes many of the biggest problems.

Was emotional intelligence a substantive part of your education? Probably not. A recent Wall Street

Journal special report on business schools concluded: "The major business schools produce graduates with analytical horsepower and solid command of the basics – finance, marketing and strategy. But soft skills such as communication, leadership and a team mentality sometimes receive cursory treatment."

Few people have set out to systematically, intentionally, and comprehensively develop their emotional selves, so it represents a great challenge and a huge opportunity.

What Kind of Leader Are You?

What does leadership mean to you? And what role do people and emotions play in it?

The importance you place on emotional intelligence will depend on the kind of leader you choose to be. There are dozens of definitions of leadership – some about setting direction, some about marshaling force, some about engaging and inspiring. I believe leadership is engaging people to go further and do better than they could on their own. It's about setting direction, and setting a context for people to do the "impossible."

In the last few years there have been a flurry of books about a new kind of leadership. The age of the Knowledge Worker, the Flat Earth, and the Global War on Terror demand a particular kind of leadership. From Drucker to Bennis, Covey to Blanchard, leadership gurus are calling for a more

> *No doubt emotional intelligence is more rare than book smarts, but my experience says it is actually more important in the making of a leader.*
>
> *— Jack Welch*[5]

subtle, relationship-centered leadership.[4] Even die-hard charismatics like former GE CEO Jack Welch are identifying that managing emotional assets is mission-critical for today's leader.

Why is that? Perhaps people are simply less compliant than 50 years ago. They are not loyal to their businesses (and businesses are not loyal to them). They are increasingly mobile and entrepreneurial – in California and all of the US, for example, the last decades have shown an explosive growth in high potential employees going independent.[6] Even more than that, it's because business today is mind-bogglingly complex. Supply chains that span the planet, delivery models moving a mile a second, and innovation faster than anything humanity could even imagine 100 years ago. Coupled with a spiraling geopolitical quagmire, weapons for the taking, weather changes, and diminishing natural resources, we've got a challenging context.

What kind of leader can navigate through it? What inner resources do you need? Some combination of great courage and mild insanity, probably. What else? What do you need to help your people be and do their best in this context? Here are ideas from three thought leaders:

> "Your foremost job as leader is to take charge of your own energy, and then orchestrate the energy of others."
> – Peter Drucker

> "Management is getting people to do what needs to be done. Leadership is getting people to want to do what needs to be done. Managers push. Leaders pull. Managers command. Leaders communicate."
> –Warren Bennis

> "Leaders enroll people to create a better future."
> – Marcus Buckingham

All three have to do with creating commitment – not just telling, but inspiring, engaging, enrolling, communicating, energizing. Starting with yourself, creating a new kind of force. One woven of thousands of careful interactions between people – not just determined to get work done, but deeply committed to bringing out the best in one another. Genuinely caring. Listening. Respecting. Challenging. Trusting.

Clearly there is more to exceptional performance than being effective with emotions. But equally clearly, if you accept that leadership includes inspiring commitment, reading subtle cues, and finding your own best wisdom, dealing with emotions is an important part of your success.

Another Book on Emotional Intelligence?

There are several fabulous books on emotional intelligence – and several mediocre ones as well. What's different about this one?

My team and I did not start out trying to write books. We started out to share the best practices from our lifetime of teaching. The chairman of my organization, Karen McCown, began teaching people these skills in 1967. My mentor and the President of Six Seconds, Anabel Jensen, was a teacher for 30 years. I was a teacher, and I still see myself as a teacher.

We started a not-for-profit organization called Six Seconds EQ Network in 1997. Since then, 100% of my time has been teaching people all over the world the skills of emotional intelligence. I've done trainings in all kinds of organizations from financial services to the military to schools to hospitals. I've helped start emotional intelligence initiatives in two dozen countries. And I help lead the world's largest network of emotional intelligence advocates, researchers, and practitioners.

This book draws on that broad base of work, and attempts to make it simple and relevant for leaders. What you'll read here is proven both in research and practice, drawing on a serious body of work that's changed the way many people live and lead.

It's my view that people learn these skills through their real-world interactions. To expedite the process, Six Seconds provides transformational learning experiences, and we work with people as they go to implement their new awareness in their daily practice. But a good book can get you started, give you some new ideas to experiment with, and, hopefully, get you inspired to take some new risks.

So whether the whole concept of "emotional intelligence" is new to you, or you've been working on these competencies for years, this book is intended to provide you with data, examples, metaphors, and practical tools you can use to improve your emotional competence, your leadership success, and your life.

Notes for Chapter One

1   Names in quotes: Throughout the book I have used real stories of leaders to help illustrate key points. To avoid embarrassing anyone, I've changed some of the names – these appear in quotes, such as "Carl."

2   How long has the "emotions are bad" paradigm existed?   The first reference I've seen is from the Latin poet, Publilius Syrus; in the 1st century, BC he wrote, "Rule your feelings, lest your feelings rule you."

3   Throughout the book I will cite research on the brain, emotions, cognition, and psychology. With the advent of new brain-imaging technologies, today scientists can literally see the brain at work.

4   Relationship-Centered Leadership: Tom Wojick, a member of the Six Seconds' Network, developed a model for Relationship-Centered Leadership (RCL) which he presented at our NexusEQ Conference Orlando, 2004.

5   Wall Street Journal, January 23, 2004

6   A great deal has been written about this trend, such as Daniel Pink's *Free Agent Nation*.

Chapter Two

Breakthrough Thinking:
Emotions are Assets

"Everyone knows" that emotions are in the way of thinking. Good, strong decisions are made with clear intellect, with our reason unclouded by the messy confusion of emotion. Right?

We've all experienced this. We get upset and we make a decision to speak harshly to someone, then we regret it. We feel that we really like someone and we give too much away in a negotiation. Later we look back and say, "Emotion was in the way."

This view has been a part of Western thought for thousands of years. In the 1st Century BC author Publilius Syrus wrote, "Rule your feelings, lest your feelings rule you." This view is frequently expressed in business today; for example an otherwise good book called *Contagious Success* (2005), states over and over, "To think critically, people have to get their emotions out of the way."[1]

Most of us have been taught, "Leave emotion out of it." We've struggled to ignore our feelings, and we've become

There can be no knowledge without emotion. We may be aware of a truth, yet until we have felt its force, it is not ours. To the cognition of the brain must be added the experience of the soul.

Arnold Bennett (1867-1931)

skilled at dismissing emotion as weak and irrelevant. We've successfully adopted this view of emotion.

The problem is, this view is wrong.

The rest of this book will show how emotions can be assets that help us make optimal decisions, be and do our very best, form highly effective relationships, and create teams and organizations that build enduring value.

Here are three facts that, taken together, show why emotions are actually one of our greatest assets.

1. Emotions exist. We all have them, all the time. Using PET and fMRI scanning,[2] scientists can show emotions at work on the brain in real time. Emotions are chemicals within our bodies and brains, there are specific neurobiological structures that essentially all healthy people have. The chemicals are called "neuropeptides;" they are a type of neurotransmitter that carries emotional signals through our bodies. These chemicals are constantly being formed (primarily in our hypothalamus) from strings of proteins, and every person has the same kinds of chemicals.

2. Emotions affect us. The way we feel influences the way we think and act. When we are in "bad moods" or "good moods" we notice different aspects of the environment around us – and we actually recall and form memories that are consistent with the feelings. In fact, the very structures we use for "thinking" and for "feeling" are totally intertwined – the same kinds of chemicals and cells are

Figure 2.1: Emotional Intelligence Predicts Success

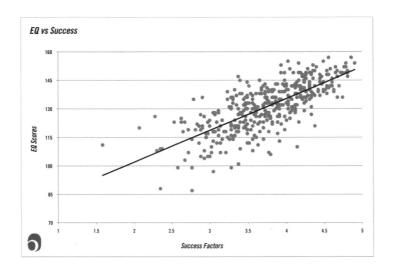

Over 54% of variation in "Success" is predicted by EQ scores (measured using the Six Seconds Emotional Intelligence Assessment - or SEI).

Visually, you can see these two variables, EQ & success, are moving together.

Success is a combination of Career Advancement + Effective Decisions + Effectiveness + Good Family Relationships + Financial Security + Good Health + Ability to Influence + Quality of Life + Professional & Personal Relationships.

involved in analytical thought and in feeling. We literally cannot separate them. As Dr. Antonio Damasio has shown, when people have damage to their emotional centers, they actually cannot make choices. Damasio wrote, "emotions are enmeshed in the networks of reason," in other words, emotions and thinking are not two different structures, they are part of the same whole.[3]

3. Emotions are data and energy. Darwin proposed an evolutionary value of emotions as a way to help us communicate. Humans are pack animals. Our species developed over millennia to work in groups, and we work in groups today. As pack animals, we need very quick ways of assessing others in the pack, of "reading" others and finding our way. Emotional expressions tell us who to approach, who to avoid. They tell us what we like and don't like. They tell us when we are living in concert with our values and when we are breaking them. At a neurobiological level, emotions are literally information and energy. The chemicals of emotion are messengers and they carry an electric charge; when we change emotional states we actually experience the energy of emotions. In fact, the molecules of emotion regulate the electrochemistry of the whole body, affecting the electrical set point of every one of our cells.[4] For example, when confronted with a major challenge, most people experience some loss of energy and drive; then when they begin to find a solution the feelings change and they get excited and full of energy.

So if emotions are there, they affect us, and they contain both data and energy, the choice is pretty simple: We can ignore them or use them. Emotions affect decision making, they affect how we engage and influence others, and they affect our own energy. In turn this changes how we are and what we accomplish as a leader and as a person. It's as if we're on raft being driven by a river. We can hang out on the raft and ignore the river and end up being tossed around. Or we can get our hands and feet wet and assert a great deal of influence on the way the raft moves.

And yet, we have all experienced how emotions can escalate and then how we can make bad decisions when we're highly emotional. We've experienced that emotions seem to cloud our thinking. We've experienced that emotions can be confusing and hard to manage.

Perhaps the problem is not emotions. Perhaps the problem is a lack of training. Growing up in a highly educated family in California, I had over 2,000 hours of formal training and practice at mathematics before I was 20 years old. Since my biological parents are both mathematicians, there were thousands of additional hours of informal practice. In college, I took one psychology class, and less than 10 hours of that class were specifically focused on understanding emotions. How many hours of formal training have you had in understanding and using emotions?

Does it Matter?

In the business case later in the book, I'll show you how innovative organizations are already increasing economic value through EQ in sales, leadership, and team performance. Companies like L'Oreal increasing profits by over $2.5 million by using EQ to hire more effective salespeople or American Express Financial Advisors yielding a gain of over 2% in sales from a 2-day EQ training.

What about you and your own success? What evidence is there that developing emotional intelligence will benefit you?

In an international study of 665 participants from entry- to C-level in a wide variety of industries, we found that emotional intelligence predicts almost 55% of key success factors.

This research shows that EQ is a critical ingredient in personal success – and may explain why developing EQ in organizations has so much value.

Fear and Anger

Two of our primal, survival oriented, driving emotions are fear and anger. Because they are such strong and challenging feelings, I'd like to use them as examples of how emotions can actually help us, how even "bad" feelings can be assets.

Fear and anger are usually seen as negative emotions, and people often speak and write about overcoming or minimizing them. It's easy to understand this perspective – I certainly dislike feeling very angry, it seems dangerous

*Fear is a question:
What are you afraid of, and why? Just as the seed
of health is in illness, because illness contains
information, your fears are a treasure house of
self-knowledge if you explore them.*

Marilyn Ferguson
(author, and editor of Brain/Mind Bulletin)

and risky. Fear is incredibly unpleasant; I intensely dislike the helplessness that comes when I feel afraid. Yet, what if these emotions are actually helpful advisors encouraging us to focus and analyze?

Think about a time when you were afraid – you might not like to call it fear, because fear is associated with weakness. Recognizing fear as fear requires real strength and courage, but the social convention is that "real men" and "big girls" are not "supposed to be afraid." We've demonized fear, so it might be easier to think of a time you were very concerned, worried, or anxious (they are all variations of fear).

I was running the first NexusEQ international conference on emotional intelligence and we were far behind plan on registrations. This was one of the largest projects our organization had taken on, and I was the one who'd pushed for it, calling in all kinds of favors from the absolutely top people in our field. The hotel and conference center deposits were all on my credit card, and if we didn't get enough signups the financial damage could have closed our organization. I had many sleepless nights and intense conversations – and over a few weeks I bit my nails to the quick. It's very unpleasant to remember those feelings and easy to see them as "bad," especially considering how I needed to be upbeat, energetic, and optimistic to bring people into the event as speakers, partners, and participants.

It feels bad – so it must be bad, right?

As you're sitting remembering one of these unpleasant

experiences, consider this proposal:

> What if these emotions are not bad for you, they are not destructive, and they are not negative. Rather, they are a source of vital information and protection. And they can be challenging.

Fear's Warning

When you touch a hot stove, it hurts. It's your body's way of saying, "**Hey!** Don't touch that!!!" So while it hurts, is that sensitivity negative or bad? It does not feel good to be burned, so we learn to avoid the hot stove. In the same way, fear is a message to help us avoid danger.

At its essence, fear is a message of uncertainty. It is a warning that there is a potential risk. The risk may be obvious (as in the fear of heights), or it may be more veiled (as in the fear of having a child). Sometimes people make this distinction between clear and generalized fears as "rational fear" and "irrational fear;" since fear is inherently non-rational, that may be a misleading differentiation. Rather, it is useful to see that there are fears we understand, and fears we don't.

To understand fear, we need to know what uncertainty is causing the fear. In the months before that conference, my fear was warning me that I did not have some essential information.

In the midst of the uncertainty, it is easy to become distracted from the real question; the fear brings in all kinds of other questions, doubts, and past experiences. Remember, feelings are self-reinforcing – when you feel fear, you recall memories and notice stimuli that reinforce the feeling. Moreover, fear is uncomfortable, so most of us try to avoid the feeling, and it ends up eating away at us in the background.

On the other hand, if you can remember that emotions contain data and energy, that there is wisdom in feeling, then you can benefit from it. Fear is a question. It's a question about risk, about concern, about the unknown, about commitment. In the case of that conference, the fear was asking me, "Do you really mean it." "Do you really mean to do something new, and very public, and very financially risky?" When I listened to the fear, it helped me.

Listening to the fear I was able to assess the real risk and my own commitment to overcome the risk. When I answered fear's question, I became fully committed to the event and its success and left "no stone unturned" to get our audience. It turns out we had been defrauded by a mailing service, and 80,000 brochures had gone into the trash instead of the mail. Nonetheless, we ended up with 500 people at the conference, making it the largest emotional intelligence conference in the world to date and fully one quarter of the participant evaluations gave it highest marks, many saying "This is by far the best conference I've attended in my career." Fear helped make it so.

Anger Kills?

Anger also has a bad reputation. I know that I've done

*If you burn your hand
on a hot stove,
does that mean
stoves are bad?*

*If you get lost
reading a map,
does that mean
maps tell us
nothing useful?*

stupid things when angry, so it is easy to see anger as destructive and negative. An hour of watching the news is enough to convince even the most emotion-friendly person that anger is at the root of all kinds of troubles.

Or is it?

Like fear, anger serves a useful purpose. Fear asks, "Are you sure?" Anger asks, "Will you take action?" Think of all the people who were angry about civil rights. About the tyranny of monarchies. Or, in more mundane angers, how about feeling so frustrated with those too-tight pants that you finally started exercising? Or so angry about tar-stained teeth that you finally quit smoking? Even anger about being told "you can't" that led you to prove you can?

Anger means "there is something I don't like about the situation," or, "my way was blocked." As with fear, the challenge is to identify that "something." Once we listen to the message, the feeling diminishes, and we have a clear course of action.

Unfortunately, like fear, anger feeds on itself when you are not clear. The generalized sense of frustration leads us to see more and more that frustrates us, and anger builds because the essential discomfort remains. Like a tiny thorn that leads to a terrible wound, the minor irritation escalates from neglect.

Everything In Moderation

These positive emotions become dangerous when they

escalate. Anger escalates to rage, fear escalates to terror. Both trigger the same kind of "fight, freeze, or flight" reaction – a core survival mechanism (I'll explain this in the "Fight or Flow" section of the book). In that crisis reaction, we **don't care** about the long-term. We forget about consequences and do anything to survive. We'll "hit back first" to destroy the risk, we'll become immobilized to hide from the risk, or we'll run to avoid it.

Yet even these extreme reactions are examples of the intelligence of our emotions. They are interpreting a situation and creating a conclusion working to keep us alive. The problem is that for most of us, *this intelligence is not trained well,* and in such challenging moments our strong emotions lead us to unproductive, dangerous, and even destructive actions.

So how does something so positive turn dangerous? Imagine these emotions are like an ignored child. Yesterday I watched my daughter, Emma, struggle with anger. She did not like what we'd told her, and so she began to protest. We did not listen to the protests, so she got louder. Finally, she picked up an expensive toy and threw it – suddenly, she got attention (perhaps even more than she wanted).

In the same way, we all experience anger or fear, and, conditioned to see them as negative, we ignore the feelings. In the case of fear, we ignore the message that we're not certain. The fear escalates to get our attention, and pretty soon we've got a generalized sense of dread, or even terror – but we don't know where it came from.

Who's Driving?

While some people talk about "emotional intelligence" as a way of being "smart in the way we control our emotions," this view misses the real point. Emotional intelligence is about how **our emotions are smart all by themselves**. Emotions are a system of processing information and drawing conclusions. They guide us and help us.

If a person tries to follow a map and gets lost, we don't assume that the map is bad, nor do we assume the person is broken. Instead, it is most likely that he just has not developed enough skill at map reading. With some training, his "map intelligence" can help him get where he's going. Likewise, many people have not developed or trained the intelligence of their emotions, and they'd gain great benefit from developing this capacity.

The terrible irony is that the more we seek to diminish and ignore our emotions, the more desperate they become to deliver their messages. We go to war within ourselves, our energy is consumed, and our decision making is impaired. Like any system, this dysfunctional relationship with emotions may "work ok" in day-to-day life. But what happens when the threats and fears pile up? When the world becomes less predictable, feels more overwhelming? Suddenly, the dysfunction becomes dangerous, and the war expands to consume us.

The alternative is to learn about emotions and form a real alliance with our own feelings. To attend to them as we listen to any good advisor – not blindly, not unconditionally, but carefully and respectfully. The heart of emotional intelligence is recognizing that there is wisdom in feelings – and we can access that wisdom so we can be and do our best.

"Forming an alliance with feelings" is a key discovery for many people. Carol is a teacher and an executive; she runs a treatment center helping First Nations' teens recover from solvent addiction – one of the first centers of its kind in the world. A wise and deep person, Carol has transformed adversity into strength – for her own healing, for the healing of her clients, and for the healing of her community and nation. She is a truly remarkable woman; she is someone I think about when I need a role model for courageous commitment.

At one of our advanced Certification trainings, Carol participated in an exercise about building an alliance with her feelings. Essentially it is a process in which we facilitate the participant to have a meeting where she asks different feelings important questions. The premise is that our feelings are trying to help us, so if we listen to them we can benefit – and the emotions will automatically transform into energy to help us.

Six months later I saw Carol. She said she felt healthier, stronger, and more deeply committed than she had in years – and she'd lost 50 pounds. I was so excited for her, I asked what happened – I didn't make the connection at all. "Don't you remember that exercise where we used our feelings as advisors?" she asked. "It's changed the way I relate to my emotions – I'm not battling myself anymore."

Chapter Two Recap

Key Concept:

Conventional wisdom is that emotions destroy logic – new evidence in neuroscience shows that the opposite is true. Emotions are essential to decision making.

Related Reading:

Descartes Error, Antonio Damasio[3]

The Wisdom in Feeling, Lisa Feldman Barret and Peter Salovey[5]

Key Practice:

Form an alliance with feelings. Don't ignore them. On the other hand, don't give them too much weight. Just as you would with any advisor, listen to their messages and evaluate that point of view.

Chapter Two Notes

1   Annuncio, Susan (2005). *Contagious Success.*

2   PET (positron emission tomography) can show which areas of the brain are active. fMRI (functional magnetic resonance imaging) shows, almost in real-time, shifting brain activity as blood moves toward areas of the brain that are more active.

3   Damasio, Antonio (1994), *Descartes' Error: Emotion, Reason, and the Human Brain,* Avon Books.

4   For more on the function of emotions, see Candace Pert's work, including *Molecules of Emotion.* There are two interviews with her on www.6seconds. org - including one called "The Physics of Emotion" which explores this topic. Pert is neuroscientist now working to cure AIDS. She was a chief of brain science at the National Institutes of Health and a professor at Georgetown Medical School, and she is a member of Six Seconds' Advisory Board.

5   Feldman Barrett, L., & Salovey, P. (Eds.). (2002). *The Wisdom in Feeling: Psychological Processes in Emotional Intelligence.* New York: Guilford Press.

Chapter Three

Business Case for EQ: Emotions on the Bottom Line[1]

There are many pressures coming together to require a new way of running a successful business. When I interviewed Daniel Pink about his book, *A Whole New Mind*; he made the case that consumers and employees want something more than utility at a good price.

According to Pink, the business challenge begins with a changing marketplace, and continues with a new generation workforce. Pink says businesses will find it increasingly challenging to hold marketshare, but there is a solution. "Many consumers in the West have had their basic material functional needs satisfied or over satisfied. The way you stand out in a crowded marketplace is to appeal to spirituality, emotion, aesthetics, and so forth."[2]

The abundance of the current Western economy translates to a glutted market. With a dozen places for gourmet coffee, why turn to Starbucks? With more cars owned in America than there are drivers, why will someone buy a Prius? Pink says "this puts a premium on aesthetic, emotional, and even spiritual aspects of goods and services," which is driving a trend Pink calls the accelerated search for meaning.

In addition to Pink's perspective, I would contend that there are several key drivers that, taken together, present a new challenge for leaders.

In the Churn

While we'd all like to have a clear and compelling plan for enduring success, I have yet to meet a leader that's got it dialed. While some organizations are mostly functional and many are mostly in chaos, all the organizations where I've had an opportunity to consult are struggling to find their feet in a uniquely challenging context. They are in the "churn." It's not just change, it's an uncertainty about how to change, how to cope. There's a certain amount of flailing going on, and especially those in the middle of organizations are feeling the pressure.

In this state of rapid and confusing change, shifting strategy, and sometimes chaos, there are brutal pressures driving leaders and organizations. In the face of challenge, I contend, emotional intelligence skills become even more vital. Some of these pressures include:

- Rapid Pace of Innovation: Incredibly short cycle times and technology life-cycles require an unprecedented ability to adapt and innovate. The emotional climate in the organization can sustain or sabotage this flexibility.

- Globalization: More complex supply chains, cross-cultural communication, distributed teams, and extremely thin profit margins from global competition creates a need for leaders to be more careful and balanced. A little drag from interpersonal tension creates a major loss. At the same time there is a lot of capital available in new markets. Unsure how to compete in this context, organizations are acquiring one another left and right.

- War for Talent: One has only to look at the headlines about Google and Microsoft battling for top engineers to see the future of this trend. In an era when people are extremely mobile or can telecommute across the globe, talented people write their own tickets. If the workplace is unpleasant or the business isn't fulfilling a meaningful vision, top talent will quickly move. For example, recently we conducted a small study with a group of nurses leading an important change in their hospital, the kind of employees an organization really needs to keep. When asked why they stay working, their number one response was relationships, closely followed by their perception that this hospital allowed them to pursue important, meaningful work.

- Transparency: In the wake of 2009 fall of Wallstreet, and similar collapses all over the globe, investors and regulators are starting to pay more attention. Organizations are required to disclose more information. Boards are required to sign that they've read the disclosures. Mistakes are broadcast in seconds on Twitter. So leaders are under increased scrutiny.

Top Issues @ Work

Leaders are increasingly concerned with finding and keeping good people – especially in a time when they are expected to "do more with less."[4]

Engaging Talent

"Finding, hiring, and keeping talented individuals"

"Developing talent – both internally and through finding and attracting good people – and equipping them for success"

"Recruiting, developing and most importantly retaining top quality experts"

Under Pressure

"Increased work responsibilities with less dollars"

"Lack of time to do an adequate job"

"Too little time to talk to colleagues"

"Managing increasing complexity, competition and regulation"

"Inadequate budgets"

Our Workplace Issues Survey tracks changing views of pressure at work and the ways leaders see emotional intelligence as a resource for addressing their challenges.

They need to make good decisions and carefully engage their people in the process rather than reacting to the pressures, hiding issues, and increasing duplicity.

• Fluctuating Value: Where a hundred years ago the stock market was the providence of a few professional investors, the internet has made it easy for a huge cross-section of society to buy, and watch, stock. As we've seen in the last decade, stock prices seem only marginally connected to good strategy and organizational effectiveness – they seem to be much more driven by perception, feelings, and even uncontrollable factors such as rumors of policy changes by foreign governments (e.g., a rumor in China drives a 10% drop in the S&P). One result is an incredibly short-sighted vision of success: Rather than a focus on enduring value, many leaders are pushed hard to focus on this quarter, this month, this week, and even this hour. Great decisions, however, require a balance between what's urgent and what's truly important. All too often I've heard leaders say that while they recognize the unequivocal need to change the way their organization treats people, they can't afford it now. **Yet somehow exceptional leaders are able to hold off the wolves and create a culture where failure is part of learning, where people are truly valued, and success is about winning the marathon – not the 100 meter sprint.**

What's the net effect? I suspect that you're feeling the pain of uncertainty and chaos. In the last 10 years I have not spoken to a single leader who says, "Yah, things here are pretty stable."

So, it's no wonder some visionary leaders are looking around and saying, "we're in a new situation – we need new tools." This is one reason emotional intelligence has become so popular. World-leading organizations from HSBC to Federal Express, from the US Marine Corps to Almaraii, are experimenting with emotional intelligence as a component of competitive advantage and as a way to cope with unprecedented labor and market pressures.

What's driving this interest? Is emotional intelligence "just a fad," or does the science offer new insight and tools that genuinely affect performance? And if EQ is so important, how do leaders find their way to the value amidst the hype?

The Harvard Business Review (HBR), one of the most prestigious sources of business-best-practice, has released several articles on emotional intelligence. Their 1997 article on EQ by psychologist and author Daniel Goleman ranks as their most requested article ever. This popularity led the HBR to re-examine the data on emotional intelligence again in 2003. Their conclusion:

"In hard times, the soft stuff often goes away. But emotional intelligence, it turns out, isn't so soft. If emotional obliviousness jeopardizes your ability to perform, fend off aggressors, or be compassionate in a crisis, no amount of attention to the bottom line will protect your career. Emotional intelligence isn't a luxury you can dispense with in tough times. It's a basic tool that, deployed with finesse, is the key to professional success."[3]

As "emotional intelligence" becomes part of mainstream vocabulary (at this point there are 9.9 million hits on Google, and 293,000 results on Google's book search), leaders are increasingly considering how this concept brings value.

In a recent study, when asked "What are the top issues you face at work?" leaders identified that 76% are on the people/relational side, and only 24% on the finance/technical side. Among these respondents, a massive 89% identify EQ as "highly important" or "essential" to meeting their organizations' top challenges.[4]

Your organization is made of people, processes, and property. For a long time, "common wisdom" has been that returns come from investing in the latter two. Yet, in the last decades, a flood of research has challenged that assumption and is increasingly proving that a company's **people are the differentiating factor**. Since emotional intelligence is all about "people smarts" – about relating to yourself and others – it's no surprise that EQ plays a major role in this dimension.

Leadership and Financial Performance: The Bottom Line Perspective

As I wrote earlier, a world-class leader must excel in many areas. It takes a special mix of talents to excel in any organization, and great leaders must be exceptionally competent. When I visit business schools, I see them doing a solid job turning out people who understand markets and spreadsheets. But what leaders tell me is their biggest challenges are with people. In particular, dealing with

Figure 3.1: EQ Performance Chain

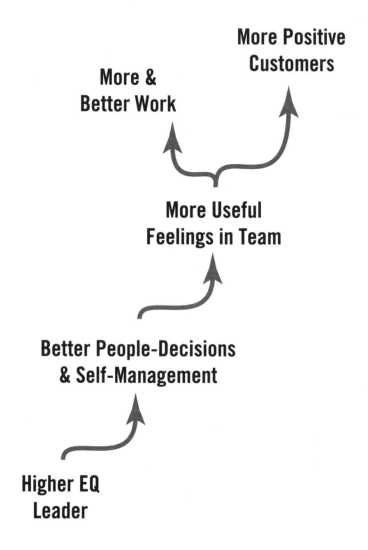

Emotional intelligence helps leaders interact in a way that shapes a positive emotional context, or climate. In turn, this drives employees and their interactions with customers.

the complexities of their people and sustaining their own energy.

Almost a third of someone's productivity can be attributed to four "human" factors. In an international study I ran with leaders, 28% of productivity is predicted by the presence of useful feedback, choice in work, seeing the value of the work, and having a positive climate.[5] It seems likely that an emotionally intelligent leader will more effectively address these human needs.

In *Working With Emotional Intelligence*, Daniel Goleman reported that 80-90% of the competencies that differentiate top performers are in the domain of emotional intelligence.[6] While IQ and other factors are important, it's clear that emotional intelligence is essential to optimal performance. Emotional Intelligence is more than twice as predictive of business performance than purely cognitive intelligence and is more predictive of business performance than are employee skill, knowledge and expertise.[7]

Numerous studies explore the financial implication of emotional intelligence; particularly how higher EQ leaders produce more powerful business results. One such study tested 186 executives on EQ and compared their scores with their company's profitability; leaders who scored higher in key aspects of emotional intelligence (including empathy and accurate self-awareness) were more likely to be highly profitable.[8]

The Harvard Business Review recently reminded leaders that their excellence begins and ends with their inner resources:

"Executives who fail to develop self-awareness risk falling into an emotionally deadening routine that threatens their true selves. Indeed a reluctance to explore your inner landscape not only weakens your own motivation but can also corrode your ability to inspire others."[9]

In the last century, "inspiring others" might have looked like Donald Trump playing the tough leader in The Apprentice. But in real organizations today, leaders face a much more complex challenge of inspiration. Again, the Gallup findings indicate that almost 3/4ths of the workforce is disengaged. Leaders who use their emotional resources to foster "engagement" (a sense of caring and commitment) deliver significant bottom-line results.

Teams with higher engagement are:

- 50% more likely to have lower turnover.
- 56% more likely to have higher-than-average customer loyalty.
- 38% more likely to have above-average productivity.
- 27% more likely to report higher profitability.[10]

So do emotionally intelligent leaders create more effective teams, or are "business smarts" and traditional intelligence all it takes? In a study of relationships between emotional intelligence and leadership, 261 members of the British Royal Navy were administered measures of intellectual competency, managerial competency, emotional intelligence competency, overall performance, and personality.[11] Participants in the study were divided into two levels of seniority, Officers and Ratings (non-officers). The results broadly illustrated the importance of emotional intelligence in predicting leadership trends. For example, compared to both managerial and IQ competencies, the EQ competencies were better able to predict:

- Overall performance

- Leadership

Further, EQ competencies made a greater contribution to leadership and performance at higher levels of the organization (i.e., EQ mattered even more for senior officers).

One key challenge in emotional intelligence research is to isolate the effect of EQ from other factors. Clarke (2010), worked to assess the impact of specific emotional intelligence skills above and beyond differences in personality and general intelligence. The study of project managers found those with higher EQ (particularly emotional awareness and understanding emotions) were linked to improved teamwork and more effective handling of conflict.[12] A similar finding occurred in a study of 81 technology professionals in India where EQ was linked to resolving conflicts in a manner that supported mutual gain.[13]

These correlations can also be linked to the bottom line. In a compelling study of one of the UK's largest restaurant groups, there was clear evidence that emotionally intelligent leaders were more effective. Managers high in emotional intelligence had restaurants that outperformed others in terms of increased guest satisfaction, lower turnover, and 34% greater profit growth.[14]

The link between EQ and leadership was also clear at PepsiCo. In a pilot project, executives selected for EQ competencies far outperformed their colleagues, delivering:

- 10% increase in productivity.
- 87% decrease in executive turnover ($4m).
- $3.75m added economic value.
- over 1000% return on investment.[15]

Similarly, a study of 358 leaders within Johnson and Johnson identified a strong link between superior performing leaders and emotional competence. The conclusion is powerful: "Emotional competence differentiates successful leaders."[16]

Ethical Leadership

In the wake of the 2009 economic crisis, the issues of ethnical leadership are gaining more attention. In part due to increasing demands for corporate transparency, and in part due the recognition of the terrible destruction caused by unethical business decisions, many organizations are re-evaluating the ways they ensure that leaders have the capacity to make ethical decisions.

In 2008, Kidwell and Valentine studied the link between workplace climate and ethics in the military. Perhaps unsurprisingly, they found that in a more positive workplace, people were more ethical (they were less likely to withhold effort or neglect job duties).[17] The implication is that leaders who create a more positive workplace climate will also reap the rewards of increased effort as well as increased ethics.

In a 2009 study, business students were given an assessment of emotional intelligence skills and tested to see how they evaluated their own and others' ethnical behavior. Empathy, the ability to connect with others' emotions, was correlated with the ability to recognize others' ethical decisions.[18] In other words, emotional awareness is tied to ethical awareness. One of these researchers conducted a similar experiment with physicians and nurses in a US hospital and, again, found that higher EQ scores predict higher performance in ethics.[19]

Getting Work Done

Shifting to productivity, several studies link emotional competence in individuals and leadership to the ability to get work accomplished. For example, a major sales study showed top performing sales clerks are 12 times more productive than those at the bottom and 85% more productive than an average performer. About one-third of this difference is due to technical skill and cognitive ability while two-thirds is due to emotional competence.[20]

The affect (emotional tone) of the leaders plays a major role in team performance. You can see this clearly in the way "everyone just knows" when boss is having a bad day. The way feelings spread from one person to another is called "emotional contagion."

"In a study of the influence of the contagion of mood of a group leader on group members, the positive mood of the leader positively influenced group members at both the individual and collective level with the opposite for leader's negative mood. The leader's positive mood also had a subsequent influence on group coordination and effort."[21]

In 2002, Sigal Barsade of Yale University examined the effect of emotional contagion within teams. In her experiment, a trained actor was placed within groups and directed to participate in the groups' activities while enacting varying levels of pleasantness and energy. The groups were working to assign a pay bonus; they had a fixed amount of money they could spend and had to allocate it based on a set of performance criteria.

When the actor was a negative group member, it disrupted the groups and reduced efficacy. Conversely when the actor played a positive confederate, the teams tended to show increased cooperation, fewer group conflicts, and heightened task performance.[22]

Likewise, in a similar study, Alice Isen (1993) assessed radiologists, finding positive mood enhanced their accuracy. Positive mood has a far-reaching effect on work performance, supervision, decision-making, and even on team members voluntarily acting for the good of the organization.[23]

The overall mood of the organization could be described as "organizational climate" – and a leader's EQ skills are a key ingredient in shaping the climate: In a study of randomly selected car manufacturing managers in Iran, emotional intelligence (particularly awareness of own and other's feelings) predicted the quality of the organizational climate.[24] So EQ skills affect climate – and climate affects performance; in one study, Hakan Ozcelik, Nancy Langton, Howard Aldrich, (2008) assessed 229 entrepreneurs and small business owners in Canada to see if they used emotionally intelligent behaviors in shaping the organizational climate. They followed up 18 months later, and leaders who created more positive climate had more revenue as well as increased growth.[25]

The Six Seconds' team in Italy recently conducted a similar study with a major McDonalds' supplier with similar findings. Higher EQ predicts better organizational climate which predicts better organizational performance. This is one reason we use the "Organizational Vital Signs" or "Team Vital Signs" assessments in our consulting processes – data about the climate is a bellweather of performance (see Chapter Eight for more on this).

The leader's skill with feelings has implications for many areas of performance. For example, the attitude that manager's display toward employees has a significant effect on employees' willingness to be entrepreneurial. Managers who display worry, frustration, and bewilderment undermine the entrepreneurial motivation.[26]

Incidentally, emotionally intelligent leaders are able to use a wide range of feelings effectively. In some situations a "bad mood" is more useful. For example, in the entrepreneur study above - Brundin, Patzelt, and Shepherd (2008) – the researches found that "negative moods" helped in certain high-risk situations where attention to detail is more critical. In another study, Elsbach and Barr (1999) found that people in negative moods use a more structured approach to decision-making which is effective in some problem-solving situations.[27]

Productivity is also tied to the relationship between the individual and the workplace. Almost a third of someone's productivity can be attributed to four "human" factors. 28% of productivity is predicted by the presence of useful feedback, choice in work, seeing the value of the work, and having a positive climate.[28]

In other words, if emotional intelligence helps leaders understand and meet employee's human needs, it will have a profound impact on productivity and individual success. Perhaps that's one reason why after a Motorola manufacturing facility used HeartMath's stress and EQ programs, 93% of employees had an increase in productivity.[29]

Likewise, after supervisors in a manufacturing plant received training in emotional competencies, lost-time accidents were reduced by 50%, formal grievances were reduced from an average of 15 per year to 3 per year, and the plant exceeded productivity goals by $250,000.[30]

The growing base of research consistently finds a powerful relationship between emotional intelligence and leadership effectiveness. It is not surprising, then, that experts propose that EQ may be the key to advanced understanding of leadership and social influence.[31]

Sales and Customer Loyalty: The Customer Perspective

Whatever kind of organization you run, a primary measure of success will be the way your customers perceive you. The organization's ability to attract and retain customers requires far more than customer satisfaction – as Benjamin Schneider wrote in the Sloan Management Review, to create loyal customers, organizations must endeavor for "customer delight."[32]

Just for a moment I'd like you to think about yourself as a customer. What vendors do you recommend to your friends and colleagues? Make a list of five reasons you particularly like those vendors. How many of your reasons are tied to relationship and emotional factors? Now turn that logic on your own company.

As I wrote before, you might not usually talk about it this way, but consider: How would you want your customers to feel? How about supported, respected, trusting, and therefore loyal? To achieve that emotional result, do your people need to feel? And, if your front-line staff are going to feel that way... what do their managers need to feel? Then, what skills and insights do senior managers need in order to create this kind of "emotional pipeline?"

EQ Sales Advantage

MetLife +37%

L'Oreal + $2,558,360

Sanofi-Aventis, +$2.2 mil/mo

Emotional intelligence is at the core of relationships, and a sales maxim is that "relationships are everything." Just how much do relationship factors affect sales and the customer's view of your organization? And what internal skills do your people need to create customer delight?

A powerful study by Benjamin Palmer and Sue Jennings demonstrates that the skills of emotional intelligence are worth over $2 million per month.[33] At Sanofi-Aventis, a pharmaceutical company, a group of salespeople was randomly split into a control and development group. The development group received emotional intelligence training and increased their EQ by 18% (on average), after which they out-sold the control group by an average of 12%, or $55,200 each x 40 reps = 2,208,000.00 per month better. **The company calculated that they made $6 for every dollar they invested in the training.**

At L'Oreal, sales agents selected on the basis of certain emotional competencies significantly outsold salespeople selected using the company's standard selection procedure. On an annual basis, salespeople selected on the basis of emotional competence sold $91,370 more than other salespeople did, for a net revenue increase of $2,558,360.[34]

More recently, Rozell, Pettijohn and Parker explored relationships between emotional intelligence and performance in a sample of medical device salespeople. Once again, emotional intelligence proved to be a highly reliable predictor of performance leading to the conclusion that salespeople who are positive, happy, and who perceive the "best" in situations combined with low levels of anger, negativity and the like will obtain the highest performance levels.[35]

Climate of Caring

The Six Seconds team and I worked with the Sheraton Studio City in Orlando in a very challenging business situation. They had experienced very high levels of executive turnover, their guest satisfaction scores were suffering, and they were losing market share. A new General Manager, Grant Bannen, came in and engaged us in a year-long project to improve performance.

In an initial interview about the challenges, Bannen said "I want to see more bounce in their step." I heard him clearly articulating an emotional challenge (again talking about feelings without calling them feelings). I suggested we measure that "bounce in the step" factor by assessing the organizational climate. Climate is like the combined feelings in an organization, the overall tone of the workplace. We used the Organizational Vital Signs (OVS)[36] measure to identify specific areas where the climate was not conducive.

Where "culture" means the rules to generate appropriate behavior ("how we do things here"), "climate" describes how people feel about coming to work. On the OVS, employees report their perceptions and feelings via a brief online survey; the data is distilled into five dimensions of climate in a powerful performance model including Motivation, Change, Teamwork, and Execution, with Trust at the center. The model is explained in Chapter Eight.

The leadership team and I developed a plan in response to the findings from the climate assessment that included internal efforts to improve communication with support from Six Seconds. We conducted a series of emotional intelligence trainings to foster dialogue, increase awareness of the emotional drivers of performance, and increase the team's competence in managing the emotional-side of their people. In total, the executive team had just over 20 hours of training, selected individuals had a combined total of under 20 hours of coaching, and the line staff had between 2 and 8 hours of EQ training.

The results included a dramatic increase in guest satisfaction and market share, and a significant reduction in turnover (see Figure 3.2).[37] The customer experience was so remarkable that the hotel group began sending their VIPs to this 3-star hotel rather than the 5-star they own. We held our 4th NexusEQ Conference at the Sheraton Studio City and the comments were the most positive we've had at any hotel. One delegate shared this story about an interaction that came to typify the Sheraton Studio City line staff: "I asked someone from the hotel where I could get a chocolate bar. She asked me what I liked, then told me she'd be right back. It turns out she went across the street and bought me one – unbelievable!"

Small experiences like this add up – and the hotel experienced an 8.3% increase in guest service scores. This was enough to make the property Sheraton's #1 rated vacation destination world-wide in customer service for two of the months at the end of the project. In a hotel that

Figure 3.2: Sheraton Case Study

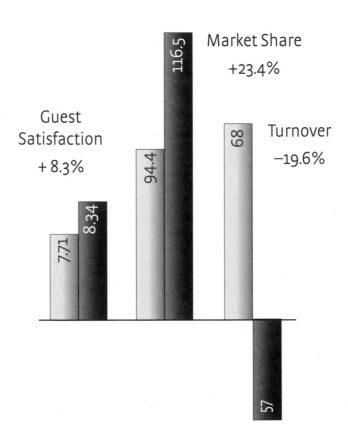

Business Results Before and After the Project

Guest Satisfaction +8.3%

7.71   8.34

Market Share +23.4%

94.4   116.5

Turnover −19.6%

68

57

After a year of EQ consulting and training, the climate and business metrics improved significantly. This tend has continued since.

was $79 per night. Again, you can invest in process and property – but at least in this case a very small investment in people made a much bigger difference (see Figure 3.2).

At the Heart of Sales Relationships

Another study examined links between emotional intelligence competencies and sales performance in 33 managers and sales agents employed at Bass Brewers in the UK. Participants took a self-assessment and were rated by their managers. They developed a measure of performance that was a composite of key outcomes and then compared the emotional intelligence scores to the performance ratings. Results included:

- Those with higher self-ratings on emotional intelligence tended to have higher overall performance.

- Those with higher emotional intelligence self-ratings also tended to perform better on product distribution, the number of new accounts sold, and employee promotions earned.

- Where manager-ratings were higher, employees tended to have overall higher performance and a larger number of new accounts sold.[38]

Again, the skills of emotional intelligence seem to be a foundation for effective relationships. The Forum Corporation on Manufacturing and Service Companies conducted extensive studies asking why customers left vendors. 30% of the reasons related to product quality and technical excellence. Meanwhile 70% related to emotional and relationship factors.[39] If you think about your own vendors – from corporate needs to personal shopping – how likely are you to remain loyal to a company that seems uncaring, disinterested, unresponsive, or distant?

Likewise, positive-psychology guru Dr. Martin Seligman studied insurance salespeople at MetLife. Dr. Seligman saw that optimism – one of Six Seconds' emotional intelligence competencies – is essential for salespeople. They are regularly rejected, and unless they have a tremendous sense of possibility they will give up. So MetLife selected salespeople on the basis of optimism. The optimists outsold other MetLife salespeople by 37%.[40]

In the early days of emotional intelligence, American Express Financial Services (now Ameriprise Financial) was looking for competitive advantage. Kate Cannon, Fred Luskin, and other consultants put together a three-day program on emotional intelligence. They focused on helping financial advisors become more aware of their own and others' emotions. In the following year, the trainees' sales exceeded untrained colleagues by 2% – which might sound minimal, but the millions of extra earnings off a three-day program convinced the company to expand EQ training.[41]

The take away from Sheraton, L'Oreal, Metlife, Morgan Stanley, and Amex cases is clear: Emotions drive people – people drive performance. Perhaps it's because "They may forget what you said, but they will never forget how you made them feel" (widely attributed to Carl W. Buechner[42]). Emotional intelligence skills seem to drive both the relationship aspects of sales, and the internal focus and drive of top sales performance. So the emotional skills of people in your organization have a profound effect on the relationship between the organization and its customers.

Attracting & Retaining Talent: The Internal Business Perspective:

Employee success is critical for the organization and for the individuals. What skills set star performers apart? What core competencies are linked to career and personal success?

In a recent study, one of the first in the Middle East, Six Seconds partnered with Dubai Knowledge Village to assess knowledge workers in this hub of the region's economic engine. In a study of 418 leaders living in the region, there is a very strong relationship between emotional intelligence skills and performance outcomes). Scores on the SEI (Six Seconds Emotional Intelligence Assessment) predict over 58% of the variation in critical professional and personal success factors (such as effectiveness, influence, relationships, financial and career status).[43]

Emotional intelligence is proving to be one of the key drivers of employee performance; higher EQ leaders build a workplace environment where team members can excel, and higher EQ team members use their business strengths more effectively and excel as star performers.

How important is EQ in distinguishing high performers? To assess this, a 2006 study at an international petroleum corporation investigated relationships between international business capability, expertise, cognitive aptitude, and emotional competencies.[44] Through interviews, surveys, and focus groups participants identified factors that differentiate average and superior performers.

Analyses of 108 interviews found that participants more frequently identify emotional intelligence factors (such as achievement motivation, empathy and self-confidence) than expertise and cognitive factors. In fact, of the 10 most commonly cited performance factors, the seven items categorized as reflecting emotionally intelligent behaviors were identified 44% of the time compared to 19% for the three factors categorized as being related to cognitive intelligence.

One reason EQ seems to be so critical to success is the effect on stress. As in many fields, healthcare is a complex and stressful environment where interpersonal interactions are of paramount importance. A study of 68 professional midwives and obstetricians in a large urban hospital found that emotional intelligence is strongly predictive of performance (66%), stress is slightly predictive (6% to 24%), and emotional intelligence is predictive of stress management (6.5%).[45] Interestingly, the most senior group in the study – those with the most supervisory and leadership responsibilities – are the ones for whom emotional intelligence made the most difference. In other words, EQ becomes increasingly important as people move up into higher levels of leadership.

These types of stressors occur in many sectors. In a study of public-sector employees, those with higher emotional intelligence found it easier to handle the perception of organizational politics and had lower abesentee rates.[46]

Star Performance Saves $190m

There is a significant cost to attracting and onboarding new employees who underperform then wash out. While estimates of hiring effectiveness range around 50%, few organizations track this hemorrhage because the costs tend to be spread over multiple budgets (recruiting, training, operations). However, the US Airforce has undertaken experiments to test the financial value of hiring people who perform. In 2009, the USAF began testing to see the effect of EQ on Pararescue Jumper candidates. A known number of candidates fail to complete the training at a cost of approximately $250,000 per trainee − if they selected candidates based on certain emotional intelligence skills, would the retention rate increase?

According to Dr. Reuven Bar-On, five key emotional intelligence skills emerged as highly predictive of course completion. Those candidates who are more "aware of their weaknesses as well as their strengths, can effectively validate their feelings and keep things in correct perspective, (are flexible and adaptive and are optimistic and positive are the ones who have the best chance of successfully completing this extremely demanding course." The net savings of selecting based on these competencies equals $190 million.[47]

Retaining Talent

In an era of increasing mobility and fierce competition for talent, attracting and retaining star employees is an urgent need. As trend-watcher Daniel Pink says, "Companies need good people more than good people need companies."[48] Turnover is one way of understanding how employees perceive an organization. Leaving the job is, of course, the last step in a long chain of diminished performance that creates distress and massive financial cost. So how does emotional intelligence affect job performance, satisfaction, and retention?

The primary reason people leave a job is relationship based. One of the key factors is the quality of the relationship between the employee and her/his supervisor/manager. As leadership guru Richard Leider says, "People don't leave companies – they leave leaders."[49]

I mentioned earlier that we did a study on reasons for high-performers leaving and reasons for staying at a hospital. This is a standard question on the OVS climate assessment, so I've got thousands of responses to these questions. Tom Wojick and I looked at 32 responses from a group of high-performing nurse leaders and graphed the results, shown in Figure 3.3.

As you can see, the "reasons for leaving" and "reasons for staying" are quite different. In other words, if you ask someone why they're leaving and then fix that problem, they still won't stay. Even more important, the reasons for staying are almost entirely tied to two factors:

Relationships and mission. People want to belong and belong to something worthwhile. This means that in the long run organizations with a healthy climate and a meaningful mission will win the war for talent.

What distinguishes relationships that lead to retention? Compelling evidence from Gallup shows that it's all about feelings. In their landmark research of over two million working Americans, the Gallup team identified three critical factors that predict if an employee is "engaged" - and engaged employees are 50% more likely to stay in their jobs.[50] The three factors:

- The employee feels cared for by their supervisor.
- They received recognition or praise during the past seven days from someone in a leadership position.
- They believe their employer is concerned about their development.[51]

These relationship factors reinforce the importance of climate; when employees feel good about coming to work they are more engaged and more effective.

To test this argument, we conducted an international study using the Organizational Vital Signs climate measure. We assessed people's feelings about the workplace and their perceptions of performance; the study included entry-level to C-level employees, both genders, and participants from 12 nations. It turns out that climate predicts 57.7% of overall performance (which we defined as effectiveness + service + retention + sustainability). In other words, the way people feel about coming to work has a massive impact on effectiveness, customer service, and retention.[52]

Figure 3.3: Retaining Talent

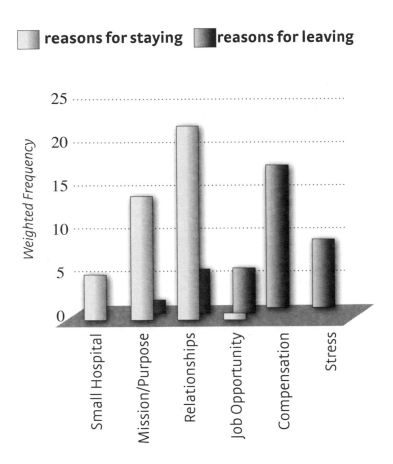

This graph shows that while you can stop someone from walking away (for a moment) by increasing compensation, if you want good people to commit, give them a connection to mission and healthy relationships.

Several other studies have documented the link between relationships in the workplace climate and people's desire to stay on the job. In the study at L'Oreal, cited previously, the "EQ Sales Agents" had 63% less turnover during the first year.

For sales reps at a computer company, those hired based on their emotional competence were 90% more likely to finish their training than those hired on other criteria. [53]

Given the emerging data, many organizations are seeking to gain this performance advantage and are using emotional intelligence testing as part of the recruitment and hiring process.

The US Air Force spends millions of dollars on recruitment every year — but their professional recruiters were only picking up an average of one recruit per month. As shown in Figure 3.4, a $10,000 investment in EQ testing let them profile the top performers, and in one year they saved $2.7 million.[54]

Ultimately, the General Accounting Office requested that the Secretary of Defense order all branches of the armed forces to adopt this procedure in recruitment and selection.[55]

Healthcare provides a prime example of the link between EQ, employee retention and the bottom line. Reports indicate 126,000 nurses are needed now to fill the United State's vacancies; today, fully 75% of all hospital vacancies are for nurses.[56] Future projections are dramatic: as fewer people enter the profession and experienced nurses near retirement, a 20% shortage in nurses is projected by 2020 – which equates to a desperate need for 400,000 nurses.[57] The US national average for turnover of nurses is 20%.

If it costs $30,000 to recruit, orient and train a nurse (estimates are up to $100,000 depending on the specialty), then a hospital staffed with only 200 nurses can expect to spend at least $1.2 million per year on new recruits. Plus, while a position is vacant, it must be filled with overtime and/or agency staff. Short staffing can also reduce the hospital's ability to admit patients which further reduces revenue – and even more importantly, can contribute to increased medical errors.

Meanwhile, in one hospital with turnover of 28%, an emotional competence and stress reduction program cut turnover by almost 50% – and within the core team turnover dropped to under 2%, saving $800,000 in less than a year.[58]

Feeling Like Working

As we discussed earlier, there are significant relationships between the climate or mood and performance. Those with higher emotional intelligence are more likely to manage their feelings – which in turn, is likely to increase job satisfaction, which is tied to both retention and performance. In a study of 523 educators in Greece, researchers showed strong links between EQ skills, affect (mood), and job satisfaction. Some 25% of the variance in mood was predicted by EQ skills, and 25% of the variation in job satisfaction was predicted by affect.[59]

Just a Fad?

People frequently ask if emotional intelligence is just a fad – another "flavor of the month," a management concept that gets attention for a month then passes into obscurity. Over the last 16 years, many "experts" have declared that the concepts of emotional intelligence are a passing fancy. The evidence is otherwise.

For example, in 2005 I chaired the 5th Annual NexusEQ Conference – delegates from 37 nations gathered in Holland to explore the current research and best practice. I regularly get emails from Masters and Doctoral students around the world, while I don't count the exact number each quarter, my impression is there are more than ever before. There are now more organizations and consultants delivering emotional intelligence programs – I know of over 400 consultancies worldwide, plus the over 3500 practitioners in the Six Seconds EQ Network. Our "Emotional Intelligence Network" group on LinkedIN is now over 40,000 members.

About 10 years ago, I often heard from clients, "Oh, emotional intelligence – we did that last year." Now I find serious organizations coming back – they are realizing that those initial introductory trainings only scratched the surface, and there are huge opportunities in actually integrating EQ into the organization. My sense is that we are just at the beginning of the growth phase of emotional

Figure 3.4: US Airforce Savings from EQ-Based Hiring

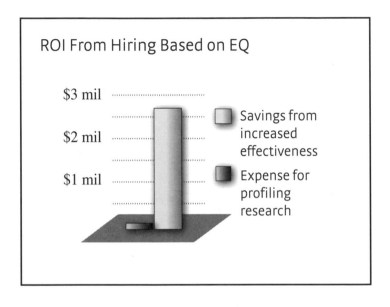

To improve the effectiveness of recruiters, an EQ measure was used to identify the characteristics of star performers. Then new recruiters were hired based on the Star Performer Profile.

intelligence. The science is getting more and more clear, the research more compelling, and best-practices more refined. Right now, many innovative organizations are testing ways of making EQ part of daily operations. As those prove out, successful organizations will put these competencies squarely in the center of their strategic planning.

Related Research

Given that EQ is so highly correlated with a range of performance outcomes, a potential to increase this competence represents tremendous opportunity.

A study conducted with one of Italy's leading information technology, engineering and management companies, Svimservice, demonstrated that even a short training program for professionals working in a highly competitive and technical environment offers significant benefits in the development of emotional intelligence competence. After a two-day training, EQ scores increased significantly.[60]

In addition to the measurable changes, anecdotally participants reported important performance changes:

> Antonella Favia (Programmer): "It was a strengthening experience that let me to enrich all my personal resources, to develop and improve my self and my communications with the others."

> Giuseppe Coppola (Analyst Designer for Web Applications): "The emotional intelligence training

helped me to understand the dynamics of human interaction in my new work place. This helped me to become more productive and better able to apply my competencies toward the team's and organization's goals."

Life Success for NFL Players

A study of 30 retired National Football League players shows that the benefits of emotional intelligence go far beyond financial performance. Many professional athletes struggle to be successful off the field. The study found that athletes with greater emotional intelligence are far more likely have good health and relationships, avoid drug/alcohol use and violence, do well at work and enjoy a high quality of life. In fact, over 60% in the variation of these "life success" factors is predicted by emotional intelligence.[61] So, if we are concerned with creating organizations and communities that are not just prosperous, but also thriving, the skills of EQ are invaluable.

A Blue Chip Investment

Bolstered by the compelling data that "soft skills" produce "hard results," some leaders are taking the challenge to create more robust, vigorous organizations – not through bricks and mortar, but by investing in people.

In an era of unprecedented business challenge, these skills matter like never before. In the words of Doug Lennick, VP of American Express Financial Advisors (now Ameriprise), emotional intelligence is the breakthrough ingredient for leaders committed to sustainable success:

> "Emotional competence is the single most important personal quality that each of us must develop and access to experience a breakthrough."[62]

The results of emotional intelligence development are evident in performance metrics – but they also turn into climate. The way employees feel changes how customers and investors feel. Emotional branding is increasingly recognized as a critical component in corporate valuation. If the leader's EQ affects internal and external perception, and perception drives both brand value and stock prices, then the emotional side of leadership is a top priority.

Perhaps the best news: Many of the companies experiencing powerful results EQ are doing so with a minimal investment: the American Express Financial Advisors project started with 12 hours of training. The Sheraton turn-around included under 24 hours of EQ training. The Air Force project cost around $10,000 in assessments (see Figure 3.4). In other words, improving organizational EQ is within reach – and the return far exceeds the investment.

Leaders are learning that emotional intelligence isn't just a new label for sales techniques or a repackaging of feel-good aphorism – they're coming to recognize emotional intelligence as a core skill-set, grounded in science, that underlies performance, and they're committing to bring these assets on board. As Andrea Jung, Chair and CEO of Avon Products, says "Emotional intelligence is in our DNA here at Avon because relationships are critical at every stage of our business."[63] With over $8 billion in sales and $1.2 billion in profits,[64] Jung is talking about an impressive strand of "DNA." The bottom line: EQ is a Blue Chip investment.

The challenge then is how to develop the capacity to manage that asset. What are the core competencies that will let leaders bring these benefits to their organizations? What capacities do team members need in order to gain this critical competitive edge? How can these tools become part of the fabric of the organization? The next step is to understand the process for putting emotional intelligence in action for yourself. Then, once you are practicing the skill and seeing how it works, you will be much more effective at integrating it into your organization.

Chapter Three Recap

Key Concept:

The way leaders handle emotions changes the way employees feel – which affects the way they do their work. Employee's feelings also change how customers feel – which affects their loyalty.

Related Reading:

Executive EQ, Robert Cooper and Ayman Sawaf

Primal Leadership, Goleman, Boyatzis, McKee

Key Practice:

Begin to monitor the "touch points" where emotional messages are passed through levels of the company and from employees to customers and other stakeholders. Keep asking, "What emotional messages are we sending?"

Chapter Three Notes

1   This chapter is adapted from our latest business case data, see www.6seconds.org/case – in 2004 we published Freedman, Everett, Wojick, "EQ at the Heart of Performance: The Business Case for Emotional Intelligence."

2   Freedman, "Leading with a Whole New Mind: Daniel Pink's Memo for Tomorrow's Leaders," August 2006 (www.6seconds.org)

3   Harvard Business Review, "Breakthrough Ideas for Tomorrow's Business Agenda," April 2003

4   Joshua Freedman, "Workplace Issues Report," Six Seconds 2008, 2010, 2012 (www.6seconds.org/wi)

5   Freedman, Joshua and Fiedeldey-Van Dijk, Carina, (2003). "The Climate for Performance: Effects of Emotional Climate on Workplace Performance," in the Vital Signs Manual, Six Seconds (www.6seconds.org/tools/vs)

6   Goleman, Daniel (1998) "Working With Emotional Intelligence." New York: Bantam

7   Gerald Mount, "The role of emotional intelligence in developing international business capability: EI provides traction." In V. Druskat, F. Sala & G. Mount (Eds.), "Linking Emotional Intelligence and Performance at Work" (pp. 97-124). Mahwah, N.J.:Lawrence Erlbaum Associates, 2006

8   Stein, S.J., Papadogiannis, P., Yip, J.A., & Sitarenios, G. (2009). "Emotional intelligence of leaders: A profile of top executives." Leadership and Organization Development Journal, 30(1), 87-101.

9   Harvard Business Review, "Breakthrough Ideas for Tomorrow's Business Agenda," April 2003

10 P. Labarre (2001). "Marcus Buckingham thinks your boss has an attitude problem." Retrieved September 16, 2008 from www.fastcompany.com

11 C Dulewicz, M Young, & V. Dulewicz, "The relevance of emotional intelligence for leadership performance." Journal of General Management, 30 (3), 71-86, 2005

12 Clarke, N. (2010). "Emotional intelligence and its relationship to transformational leadership and key project manager competences." Project Management Journal, 41(2), 5-20.

13 Godse, A.S., & Thingujam, N.S. (2010). "Perceived emotional intelligence and conflict resolution styles among information technology professionals: Testing the mediating role of personality." Singapore Management Review, 32(1), 69-83.

14 BarOn, Reuven and Orme, Geetu, (2003), reported in Orme and Langhorn, "Lessons learned from implementing EI programmes" pp 32-39, Competency & Emotional Intelligence, Volume 10, 2003

15 McClelland, D.C. (1998). "Identifying competencies with behavioural event interviews." Psychological Science, 9(5) 331 – 340

16 Cavallo, Kathleen (2002), "Emotional Competence and Leadership Excellence at Johnson & Johnson: The Emotional Intelligence and Leadership Study," Consortium for Research on Emotional Intelligence in Organizations (CREIO)

17 Kidwell, R. E. and S. R. Valentine: 2008, "Positive Group Context, Work Attitudes, and Organizational Misbehavior: The Case of Withholding Job Effort." Journal of Business Ethics. Published Online 4 June, 2008

18 Joseph, J., Berry, K., & Deshpande, S. P. (2009). "Impact of emotional intelligence and other factors on

perception of ethical behavior of peers." Journal of Business Ethics, 89, 539-546. doi: 10.1007/s10551-008-0015-7

19   Deshpande, S.P. (2009). "A study of ethical decision making by physicians and nurses in hospitals." Journal of Business Ethics, 90, 387-397.

20   Daniel Goleman, "Working With Emotional Intelligence." New York: Bantam. 1998

21   Sy, Côté, & Saavedra, 2005, as cited in Sigal Barsade & DE Gibson, "Why does affect matter in organizations?" Academy of Management Perspectives, 36-59, 2007

22   Sigal Barsade, "The ripple effect: Emotional contagion and its influence on group behavior." Administrative Science Quarterly, 47 (4), 644-675, 2002

23   Sigal Barsade & DE Gibson, "Why does affect matter in organizations?" Academy of Management Perspectives, 36-59, 2007

24   Momemi, N. (2009). "The relation between managers' emotional intelligence and the organizational climate they create." Public Personnel Management, 38(2), 35-48

25   Hakan Ozcelik, Nancy Langton, Howard Aldrich, (2008) "Doing well and doing good: The relationship between leadership practices that facilitate a positive emotional climate and organizational performance", Journal of Managerial Psychology, Vol. 23 Iss: 2, pp.186 – 203

26   Brundin, E., Patzelt, H., & Shepherd, D.A. (2008). "Managers' emotional displays and employees' willingness to act entrepreneurially." Journal of Business Venturing, 23(2), 221-243

27   K. Elsbach & P. Barr, "Effects of mood on individuals' use of structure decision protocols." Organization Science, 10 (2), 181-198, 1999

28 Joshua Freedman and Carina Fiedeldey-Van Dijk, Ph.D. (2003). "Speaking Out: What Motivates Employees to be More Productive" (www.6seconds.org)

29 HeartMath, 2003

30 Pesuric & Byham, 1996

31 F.W. Brown & D. Moshavi, "Transformational leadership and emotional intelligence: a potential pathway for an increased understanding of interpersonal influence." Journal of Organizational Behavior, 26, 867-871, 2005

32 Schneider, B (1999) "Understanding Customer Delight and Outrage," Sloan Management Review Fall. Also see, T.O. Jones and W.E. Sasser, Jr., "Why Satisfied Customers Defect," Harvard Business Review, volume 73, November-December 1995, pp. 88-99

33 Jennings, S. and Palmer, B (2007), "Enhancing Sales Performance Through Emotional Intelligence Development, Organisations & People," May 2007, Vol 14. No 2, and personal correspondence with Dr. Palmer. The salespeople in the study were selected because all were in the in the same revenue band starting at $460k/mo in sales.

34 Spencer & Spencer, 1993; Spencer, McClelland, & Kelner, 1997 (cited in Cherniss, 2003)

35 E.J. Rozell, C.E. Pettijohn & R.S. Parker (2006). "Emotional Intelligence and Dispositional Affectivity as Predictors of Performance in Sales People."

36 Organizational Vital Signs (OVS) is a validated measure of organizational climate. See www.6seconds.org/ tools/vs

37 Freedman, J (2003) "Case Study: Emotional Intelligence at the Sheraton Studio City Hotel," Six Seconds

38 M. Lloyd (2001). "Emotional intelligence and Bass Brewers Ltd." Unpublished doctoral dissertation, Nottingham Business School, The Nottingham Trent University

39 Whiteley, RC (1991), "The Customer Driven Company: Moving from Talk to Action" Addison-Wesley, pp.9-10 (Based on a 1988 survey of 2,374 customers of 14 companies by the Forum Corporation)

40 Seligman, M.E.P. (1990). "Learned Optimism," New York: Knopf

41 Cannon, Kate (1999), Conference Proceedings, NexusEQ 2000

42 This quote appears on dozens of quotation web sites, but I've not found a single reference to who "Carl W. Buechner" is or was. If you know, please email me!

43 Joshua Freedman, Jayne Morrison, Andreas Olsson (2010), "Leadership Success and Emotional Intelligence in the Middle East" (www.6seconds.org)

44 Gerald Mount. "The role of emotional intelligence in developing international business capability: EI provides traction." In V. Druskat, F. Sala & G. Mount (Eds.), "Linking Emotional Intelligence and Performance at Work" (pp. 97-124). Mahwah, N.J.:Lawrence Erlbaum Associates, 2006

45 Lorenzo Fariselli, Joshua Freedman, Massimiliano Ghini MBA, Federica Valentini. "Stress, Emotional Intelligence, & Performance in Healthcare." Six Seconds, 2008

46 Vigoda-Gadot, E., & Galit, M. (2010). "Emotions in management and the management of emotions: The impact of emotional intelligence and organizational politics on public sector employees." Public Administration Review, 72-86

47 Reuven Bar-On (2010), "New US Air Force Study:

EQ to Save $190 Million" (www.6seconds.org) and personal correspondence; study conducted with MHS (Toronto).

48 Daniel Pink, quoted in Joshua Freedman, "Leading with a Whole New Mind: Interview with Daniel Pink," www.6seconds.org, 2006

49 Leider, Richard J. (1997) "The Power of Purpose," Berrett-Koehler

50 Broder, Mark (1999) quoting Marcus Buckingham, "It's the Manager, Stupid," Fortune Magazine Oct 25

51 Buckingham, Marcus and Coffman, Curt (1999) "First, Break All the Rules: What the World's Greatest Managers Do Differently," Simon & Schuster

52 Climate and performance: This is one of many studies Six Seconds' team has conducted using Organizational Vital Signs assessment (www.6seconds.org/tools/vs). The test examines five key aspects of climate including perceptions about leadership and about trust. These findings were reported in Fiedeldey-Van Dijk, Carina and Freedman, Joshua (2004), "Measuring the Effect of Climate on Performance."

53 Hay/McBer Research and Innovation Group, 1997

54 Handley, Richard (1999), Conference Proceedings, NexusEQ 2003

55 GAO "Military Recruiting: The Department of Defense Could Improve Its Recruiter Selection and Incentive Systems," submitted to Congress January 30, 1998

56 American Hospital Association's TrendWatch (www.aha.org), June 2001

57 Buerhaus, Peter et al (2000), Journal of the American Medical Association, June 14

58 HeartMath LLC at Delnor Hospital, using a training program that includes many emotional intelligence

components, 2002

59   Kafetsios, K., & Zampetakis, L. A. (2008). "Emotional intelligence and job satisfaction: Testing the mediatory role of positive and negative affect at work." Personality and Individual Differences, 44, 712-722. doi: 10.1016/j.paid.2007.10.004

60   Lorenzo Fariselli, Joshua Freedman, Massimiliano Ghini, "White Paper: Increasing Emotional Intelligence," Six Seconds, 2006

61   Joshua Freedman and Marvin Smith, "White Paper: Emotional Intelligence for Athletes' Life Success," Six Seconds (www.6seconds.org/tools/sei/research) 2008

62   Fast Company, "How Do You Feel," June 2000

63   Harvard Business Review, "Leading by Feel," January 2004

64   Avon Annual Report, 2002

Part Two:

EQ in Action

Chapter Four

123 KCG:
A Simple Model
for Practicing
Emotional Intelligence

Six Seconds is an international organization supporting people to create positive change - everywhere, all the time. We recognize that the major barrier to change is emotional – we don't change if we don't create the right conditions in each of us, in our teams, organizations, and communities, to facilitate transformation. So, we've developed a practical, learnable, measurable process for being smarter with feelings.

We define emotional intelligence as the ability to integrate thinking and feeling to make optimal decisions. Six Seconds has developed a highly effective model for putting emotional intelligence into action in leadership and life – a simple three-step process for making emotionally intelligent choices. **These three steps will let you use emotions as assets and provide you with a way to see more clearly into the heart of people.**

Figure 4.1: The Iceberg

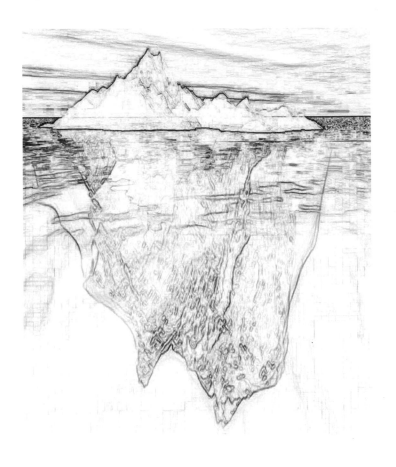

At Six Seconds, we use the iceberg to represent the importance of what's "hidden beneath the surface." Behavior is the tip of the iceberg, yet we tend to focus almost exclusively here. EQ helps you understand the drivers of behavior that live beneath the surface – which is also the most significant and powerful part of the iceberg.

Look Beneath the Surface

One of the great values of studying emotional intelligence is the insight it gives you into yourself and others. People are complex, subtle, and a lot of our behaviors just don't seem to make logical sense. But **people behave the way they do for a reason, and frequently that reason is tied to emotion.**

Imagine an iceberg, imagine a mountain of ice rising out of the water. It's huge and complex and magnificent. And, you are only looking at the $1/11^{th}$ that's above the surface. That part represents someone's behavior. The behavior you see at work and home every day.

But what is the *source* of that behavior? What influences and drives it? Those "hidden drivers" are represented by the $10/11^{ths}$ beneath the surface. Perhaps it is the part that matters most.

Likewise, the $1/11^{th}$ represents what you see of yourself on a daily basis. The $10/11^{ths}$ represents the hidden drivers that influence and shape your own performance.

There are many drivers "beneath the surface": your mental state, your physical self, your spirit, and certainly your emotions. Emotional intelligence lets you explore and understand a large part of what's hidden beneath the surface – in yourself and in others. As you come to understand these emotional drivers, you will become more able to strategically use emotions to get optimal results.

Leveraging your EQ can transform your leadership and your life. A few years ago, an HR Director from a financial services company came to our 5-day EQ training in South East Asia. "Asana" was living a highly successful life; she and her husband were both well-educated, busy executives. She was a good mother, making sure her only daughter – now a teenager - was also prepared for success. In the training program, Asana started to "dive beneath the surface" and look at what drives her. As the week went on, she began to reflect about her relationship with her daughter and the legacy she was leaving. On the fourth day she came to me full of tears, "I just wanted you to know that this morning I had the first honest conversation with my daughter that I can remember. And when we were talking, for the first time since she was little, she told me she loved me." I know Asana's personal life was changed by this experience, and I wonder how this will transform her leadership. Like a blindfold removed, Asana was seeing the 10/11^{ths} – seeing the heart.

As you develop your understanding of EQ, you will become more skilled in diving beneath the surface and seeing the magnificence and complexity of the whole iceberg. If you approach yourself and others with a real curiosity – a sense of wonder and hopefulness for knowing – you can be astounded by what you will learn and how it will help you.

To drive the metaphor home, consider the guys at the helm of the "unsinkable" Titanic. They looked at the 1/11th above the surface and drove on. But the 10/11^{ths} below the surface proved their undoing.

The Origins of Emotional Intelligence

Most people first heard the term "emotional intelligence" around 1995 with the publication of Daniel Goleman's best-selling book *Emotional Intelligence: Why It Can Matter More Than IQ*. In that work, Goleman laid out a powerful case that factors such as self-awareness, self-discipline, and empathy determine personal and professional success. He drew on the work of numerous leading scientists and authors who were working to define and measure the skills of emotional intelligence.

A global community of emotional intelligence practitioners has emerged, with consultants, researchers, trainers, and coaches implementing emotional intelligence training in all sectors of society.

Innovative businesses have begun to embrace the concept. The *Harvard Business Review* calls it "the key to professional success."[1] Schools, hospitals, and government agencies world-wide are adopting EQ practices. From elementary school students to army officers from sales execs to hotel staff, a curriculum of emotional awareness is providing a new perspective on people.

According to Dr. Goleman, it all began with two psychology professors on a summer's day in 1987. "John Mayer and Peter Salovey invented the whole field," Goleman explains, "when they were chatting about politics while painting a house." Salovey, (now Provost of Yale University) and Mayer (now Professor of Psychology at University of New Hampshire) were talking about their research on cognition

Emotional intelligence is the ability to perceive emotions, to access and generate emotions so as to assist thought, to understand emotions and emotional knowledge, and to reflectively regulate emotions so as to promote emotional and intellectual growth.

- Mayer & Salovey, 1997

and emotion, and got to discussing a politician. They wondered: How could someone so smart act so dumb? Their conclusion: Smart decision making requires more than the intellect as measured by traditional IQ.

Goleman continues the story, "And because of that conversation, they published a wonderful seminal article – but in an obscure journal. The moment I saw their concept of emotional intelligence all kinds of bells went off. And I thought, 'I have to write about this!'" With over 5 million copies in print in 30 languages, Goleman was right: The world was ready to learn about this powerful concept.[2]

Many other researchers and thought-leaders have contributed to the concept of emotional intelligence. Reuven BarOn was researching the effects of emotion on performance in late 1980s as well. In fact, in a draft of his Ph.D. dissertation he even used the term "EQ." Now researchers all around the world are refining the scientific definition and practitioners are developing models to implement the science.

Salovey and Mayer updated their definition of emotional intelligence in 1997 to more clearly focus on the abilities to perceive and use emotions as part of thinking (see inset on previous page).

Also in 1997, a group of educators met around a kitchen table in San Mateo, California. In his 1995 book, Daniel Goleman had written about our curriculum, *Self-Science*, as one of two models for how to teach emotional intelligence:

"*Self-Science* is a pioneer, an early harbinger of an idea that is spreading to schools coast to coast."[3]

Karen McCown, the author of the *Self-Science* program, had been teaching these skills for 30 years, and had formed an internationally acclaimed school based on the premise that emotional development and academic development were co-equal. Anabel Jensen (Six Seconds President) was the Executive Director of that school for 14 years; Marsha Rideout (Six Seconds Associate Director) and I were teachers there.

We looked at Salovey and Mayer's work, Goleman's models, and the science and education theory around these findings. We studied Antonio Damasio's work on emotion as central to decision making, Joe LeDoux's work on emotional reactions, and Candace Pert's findings on the neurobiological basis of emotion. We were looking for a way to distill all our experience and this extensive research into a simple model. Our concern was, and is, how people could use their emotional intelligence in leadership and life – to find more fulfillment, wholeness, health, prosperity, and purpose.

We wanted to bring all this science into a simple-but-powerful, clear model. Over years, we identified a three-step process. A path for applying emotional intelligence in leadership and life. Then we identified the specific competencies that would enable someone to take the path.

Six Seconds Model

Here are the three steps to using your emotional intelligence - we call these the three pursuits:

1 **Know Yourself** – awareness. Increasing self-awareness, recognizing patterns and feelings, lets you understand what "makes you tick" and is the first step to growth.

2 **Choose Yourself** – management. Taking ownership and responding intentionally allows you to consciously direct your thoughts, feelings, and actions (vs reacting unconsciously).

3 **Give Yourself** – purpose. Aligning your daily choices with your larger sense of meaning unlocks your full power and potential.

The model is depicted in Figure 4.2; it is presented in a circle because the three steps are cyclical. Like a propeller driving a ship, the model should "spin," it works when you Know, Choose, Give, Know, Choose, Give, Know... etc. As you spin this "EQ propeller" you will gain momentum and insight to move toward optimal decisions.

Imagine you're making a change in your company because after reading the business case in this book, you realize you're sending the wrong emotional messages to employees and, in turn, that's creating suboptimal responses from customers.

Figure 4.2: Six Seconds EQ Model

The Six Seconds Model of Emotional Intelligence is based on three action steps, or pursuits:

Know Yourself – increase awareness.

Choose Yourself – act intentionally.

Give Yourself – align with purpose.

The competencies of Know Yourself will help you see WHAT needs to change. The Choose Yourself tools will supply the HOW so you can put the change in action. The Give Yourself components will remind you and your people WHY this change is important.

At first, the term "Give Yourself" might seem "soft," but it is the key distinguishing feature that makes the Six Seconds Model transformational. When you connect your daily actions with your deepest sense of purpose, you will make the best possible decisions, develop self-mastery, and most effectively engage commitment from others. Think of giving your best, every day.

So what does it take to know yourself, choose yourself, and give yourself? What specific skills are required for success? We have identified eight fundamental competencies that are part of our training and research. They are illustrated in Figure 4.3.

Each of the eight competencies in this model is essential for putting emotional intelligence into action. These are the competencies measured by the *Six Seconds Emotional Intelligence Assessment* (see the Appendix). Each competency has value to you as a leader – and as a person. Taken together they will help you influence others, build full commitment, make great decisions, and lead and live to your highest intentions.

Throughout the rest of the book I will refer to these eight competencies and expand upon why they matter and how you can apply them.

Figure 4.3: Six Seconds EQ Model in Detail

Within the three Pursuits of the Six Seconds Model there are eight specific, learnable competencies. These are like the "muscles" that help you achieve each pursuit.

The colors are significant: Blue for reflection, red to pause, and green to GO!

Putting it in Practice

Here's an example of the model in practice: Recently my team was going through a strategic planning process and someone suggested that we make a significant change in our structure, a structure I'd developed and considered successful.

Know: At first I thought it was a bad idea, then I noticed my feelings were defensive and a little hurt.

Choose: My short-term goal was an open dialogue, so stopped myself from reacting right away. When I considered my feelings more closely I realized that my hurt was a signal that we were touching on something important to me, and I had a lot of options including: be defensive, back off, challenge my own assumptions, experiment, express my concern, or treat this as an adventure.

Give: When I considered the other people's feelings, I realized they were concerned about the organization and there was no personal attack. I thought about my real purpose, and realized that we were all actually in alignment, so I jumped on board.

In the rest of the book I will give illustrations showing how the three pursuits and eight competencies work in different aspects of leadership. But before you read more, I'd like you to test out the model and prove to yourself that this approach can really make a difference.

Exercise for Putting it in Practice

Think of a decision you have to make, or a situation you are facing right now in your work or life. Something where you could really use your full wisdom. Perhaps you have a challenge with a colleague, a new initiative you are developing, a major organizational or life change, or a similar significant opportunity? This exercise works with any decision, so it does not need to be monumental – in fact, it may be easier to start practicing with an important-but-not-critical situation.

In 30 seconds, note down the situation in a few bullet points.

·

·

·

Now apply the model.

1. Know Yourself: What are you feeling?

You always have more than one feeling, but it can be hard to identify. It may help you to focus on the situation, then notice your own body's reaction – where are you tense? How does your stomach feel, etc. Now write down some feelings. To help you, on the next page there is a list of basic emotions and some of the less and more extreme feelings that go with the emotion.

1: What are your feelings about the situation? (It is helpful to identify 2-3 +; sometimes feelings are paradoxical).

---

2. Choose Yourself: What are your options?

It can be difficult to find options when you are in reaction (e.g., when you are fighting or distressed). If you are, first pause, grab a cool glass of water, take a short break. Then, using your skills at Consequential Thinking, Navigating Emotions, Intrinsic Motivation, and Optimism, you can identify three or more choices of what you could think, feel, and do. Consider what you want to achieve in the short term, decide what results you'd like to get right now.

If you find it challenging to identify multiple options, try changing your mood by watching a funny television show, talking to a good friend, or having a walk. Often we get stuck in "this is the only way" when we're stressed, frustrated, afraid, hurt, etc. Breaking the cycle of escalation (see chapter six) lets you step out of reaction and innovate.

(form continues on page 99)

Figure 4.4: Naming Emotions

Each emotion has a wide range of variation / intensity:

Emotion	Low Intensity	High Intensity
Anger	annoyance	rage
Anticipation	interest	vigilance
Joy	serenity	ecstasy
Trust	acceptance	adoration
Fear	concern	terror
Surprise	distraction	amazement
Sadness	pensiveness	grief
Disgust	boredom	loathing

There are many different theories about emotions and lists of the "basic" emotions. This model comes from a researcher named Robert Plutchik who focused on the physiological aspects of emotion (how they work in the body). More detail on his model and emotions is in chapter five.

> 2: Get out of reaction and then identify three or more options:

3. Give Yourself: What do you TRULY want?

Empathy is an emotional response to others' emotions. What are the other people involved thinking and feeling? If you let yourself be open and a little vulnerable, what do you feel in response? Empathy is basically non-analytical, it's an openness to another's experience and perspective. Being empathic does not mean your choice should make everything feel nice for others, it just means that you are experiencing the feelings and are taking those into account. The reason empathy is part of "Give Yourself" is that it is only when you really put yourself in a kind of Servant Leader mode – when you give of yourself – that you can open yourself to another's feelings. In so doing, you gain tremendous insight and influence – but if you do it for selfish reasons, you don't get the empathy benefit. If you accept that person is doing the best they can, and set your intention to support her or him, and you truly give yourself to the person, you will gain deep understanding.

Now, reflect on your own abiding sense of purpose. Why are you in this world? What is your legacy? We will explore this more in chapter seven, and you will see why this is the hallmark of an exceptional leader.

Which of your options sustains your Noble Goal and supports the other people in the situation to be and do their best as well?

> 3: Of those options, which choice will best work with others – and line up with your own purpose?

What conclusion did you come to?

Did reflecting on the situation through these three steps help you find clarity?

Now that you've gone through these steps, can you better communicate your decision with strength and compassion?

What About Others?

Learning about the Six Seconds Model, people often notice the Three Pursuits are all about "Yourself" and they ask, "Why is it all about 'yourself'? What about others?"

Our premise is that the only person you can really change is yourself. You are the instrument of your own leadership. You are the tool. You are the lever. And if you want to change others, if you want others to behave a particular way, or feel a particular way, you will change the way you feel, think, and act. Feelings are infectious; as a leader you engender emotion in others, you set the stage for your team's feelings. In turn, those feelings change they way they perform.[4]

If the situation you explored in the Putting it in Practice exercise above had to do with other people, you probably thought a lot about them, especially in the third step. But it goes deeper. Every step of the model is about you – and you in relation to others.

When we ask you to know your own feelings and reactions, that is the way you can learn about others. Your perceptions are colored by your own feelings and reactions, so unless you are aware of yourself, you will not accurately read others.

When we ask you to reflect on your options and the consequences, you are measuring your impact on other people. You are assessing how your choices affect the world around you.

When we ask you to empathize and connect with your noble goal, we are inviting you to put yourself in balance with the rest of the world – to truly take ownership of the impact you have on others.

If you apply this model effectively, you will take care of yourself and of others. Your goal is an optimal relationship with yourself and others, and your attention to emotions will make a significant difference.

We don't see things as they are,

we see things as we are.

Anais Nin (1903 - 1977)

Chapter Four Recap

Key Concept:

The Six Seconds Model of Emotional Intelligence lets you put EQ into action in three steps: Know Yourself (be aware), Choose Yourself (manage your feelings, thoughts, and actions), Give Yourself (connect with others and with purpose).

This model works when you "spin it like a propeller" rotating through the steps in a repeating cycle.

Related Reading:

Handle with Care, **Joshua Freedman et al**

EQ from the Inside Out, **Granville D'Souza**

Key Practice:

123 KCG. When making decisions, ask yourself three questions: What am I feeling? What options do I have? What do I TRULY want? Keep repeating in a cycle to manage complex situations.

Chapter Four Notes

1   *Harvard Business Review*, "Breakthrough Ideas for Tomorrow's Business Agenda," April 2003

2   Freedman, J (2005) Interview with Daniel Goleman, NexusEQ

3   *Self-Science* is a highly effective curriculum for developing social and emotional skills. The program was launched in 1967, and the curriculum was first published in 1978. Information is online at www.6seconds.org/education/. Preparing his 1995 book, Daniel Goleman visited the Self-Science program and describes it as one of two model approaches for teaching EQ. Goleman, Daniel (2005) *Emotional Intelligence: Why It Can Matter More Than IQ*. New York: Bantam Books

4   Freedman, J (2007). "White Paper: Emotional Contagion," www.6seconds.org, San Francisco: Six Seconds

Chapter Five

Know Yourself:
The Wisdom of Feelings

When people understand how emotions function on a biological level it helps them gain a higher level of self-mastery. Earlier I discussed fear and anger, two challenging emotions, and discussed some of the "rules" that govern those feelings. Emotional literacy can grow from investigating these theories about feelings, and it also requires experiencing feelings – thinking about feelings plus feeling the feelings.

There was a wonderful VP of Finance in one of my training programs. I'll call him Stewart. Incredibly smart, very successful, great sense of humor. Trained in finance, he'd started and run several companies. Like so many others, Stewart grew up being taught that emotions were bad. All emotions. He'd rebelled enough to find that love and joy were worthwhile, but he was still having trouble with fear and anger. At one point he said to me, "When you talk about 'fear,' I don't really know what that is. I understand it intellectually, but I can't feel it." He could think about the feeling, but he had forgotten how to feel it.

EQ Competency:
Enhance Emotional Literacy

Feelings are a complex aspect of every person. This skill lets us sort out all of those feelings, name them, and begin to understand their causes and effects. It is the basic building block of emotional intelligence.

As a leader, Enhancing Emotional Literacy helps you gain important data about yourself and others, access your intuition, and master the inner landscape of emotion. Without this skill, emotions remain vague, confusing, misleading noises. Leaders who do not have Emotional Literacy are unlikely to communicate effectively with and about people, they will be surprised by others' reactions, and they might make a lot of mistakes interpreting their own and others' reactions.

Then Stewart realized it was not just fear. He was disconnected from his emotions and it was keeping him from being who he really wanted to be. While he'd experienced tremendous success, he saw that his life was somehow incomplete – and that he was beginning to pass that legacy onto his children. Moreover, while he was successful, he saw that his businesses were becoming more complex, and his current level of people-skills were inadequate to manage the growth.

He came to see that over the years he'd shut himself off from feelings. It was making it hard for him to connect with others at work and at home, and his quality of life was diminishing. It's a terrible cycle that so many of us fall into – because we've been taught that emotions (especially "negative" ones like fear, anger, sorrow, and remorse) are bad.

But neurobiologically, emotions are essential to making our brains work. Emotions give weight to ideas, they help us discern between what's true and false, they direct our attention, and they make it possible to make decisions.

The Neurobiology of Feeling

At a neurobiological level, emotions are chemicals. They are neuropeptides – a class of neurotransmitter that is made from a string of peptide proteins formed into a unique structure. Similar to hormones, the molecules of emotion flow through our brains and bodies carrying

Figure 5.1: The Limbic Brain

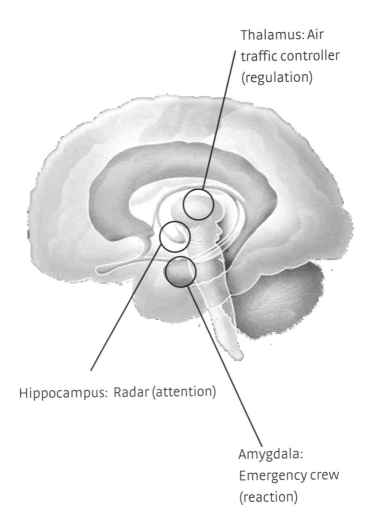

Thalamus: Air traffic controller (regulation)

Hippocampus: Radar (attention)

Amygdala: Emergency crew (reaction)

In this metaphor, the Radar (hypocampus) brings in data; the Air Traffic Control (thalamus) regulates flow of data; the Emergency Crew (amygdala) takes action when there is threat.

messages that affect many aspects of our physical and mental function.

There is a part of your brain that is, right now at this second, manufacturing these molecules (the hypothalamus). Next door, your thalamus is regulating the flow of chemical signals through your brain. As different sensory information enters, the thalamus regulates and routes that data triggering the release of different neuropeptides (see Figure 5.1).

Meanwhile, the mix of chemicals affects our perceptions. The hippocampus, in part, determines where we focus our attention and what we notice. It is stimulated by the emotion molecules to attend to different parts of our environment (internal and external). Then new sensory information enters, and again the thalamus directs those signals around the brain in a self-reinforcing system.

In other words, when we have a feeling, it causes us to notice certain things, and then those things we notice reinforce the feeling. It's a system primarily focused on survival — it causes us to hone-in on dangers, drilling in to carefully evaluate safety. Secondarily, our emotion-thinking-awareness system attends to the pleasures that can help us sustain life and reproduce.

The landscape of the brain is fascinating and complex. Our brains are chaotic systems sizzling with electricity and surging tides of chemicals. They are non-linear and always-changing. Brain cells themselves change, and the links between them move forming new pathways in an

Figure 5.2: A Synapse

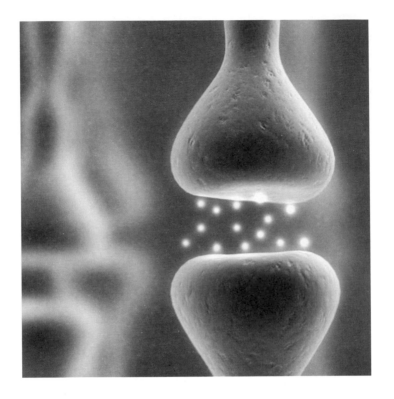

Every one of your 100 billion brain cells has numerous branching "arms," called dendrites. The dendrites come near one another: the space is a synapse.

Thoughts and feelings are made from an electrochemical "juice" that moves across the synapses. The chemicals have unique structures - like keys. The juice also carries a variable electrical charge (from 0 to about 70 volts).

intricate 3-dimensional spider web.

If you hold up a hand, you've got a model of a brain cell. The palm is the cell body, your arm is the axon, and your fingers are dendrites. Hold up another hand, and move your fingers so they are almost touching – that gap is the synapse (see Figure 5.2). Now imagine millions of these fingers interconnecting. There are between 1E14 and 1E800 synapses in every human brain (that's a 1 with between 14 and 800 zeros!)

The signals we call "thoughts" and the signals we call "feelings" are all mixed together in the brain. Electrochemical signals flow across the synapses – electrical charges (these are analog charges so they vary in intensity) and chemical molecules. The molecules each have a unique shape and structure – like a key.

There are receptor sites (locks for these chemical keys) on every cell in our body, including these brain cells (which, by the way, are not just in our brains!) The chemical message "keys" travel around in our bodily fluids and find "locks" where they fit. When the key fits, the cell is stimulated to a particular action – usually producing more chemicals that trigger other reactions. So every thought and feeling is a cascade of electrochemicals rippling through this brain-body network at lightning speed.

The structure of the network itself changes – every time we learn, for example – with dendrites linking together in different patterns to connect one "network node" with another. In addition, the receptor sites change; we actually develop more receptors depending on which kinds we use more.

So, the brain-body network is constantly changing depending on how we use it – whatever we repeat over time becomes hard-wired as the linkages and the cellular structures adapt. They don't adapt to our aspirations and dreams, they adapt to our habits – the network will adapt to whatever we think, feel, and do often.

Over millennia, this complex and elegant system has refined so that we get rich and subtle cues about navigating through the world around us. Some cues are about others – about who to trust, who to respect, who to avoid, who to love. Other cues are about ourselves and our own choices – what is moral, what is reasonable, what will protect, what will create growth.

The subtlety of emotional messages is problematic for many of us. Emotions don't just hold up signs directing us. Instead they give us signals that come almost as physical sensations (a push, a tug, a warmth, a coldness, a buzz, a dullness) each conveying nuanced indicators about how we're experiencing the world.

Decoding the Messages

So we have this complex, subtle, constantly changing system (sounds like many IT departments) – where is the user's manual? How do we learn to decode the messages of these feelings?

Just as "literacy" means knowing the letters, words, and sounds for communication, emotional literacy means knowing the basic building blocks for emotional communication. Emotional literacy is the competence to accurately recognize and understand feelings. There are two basic components to emotional literacy:

> **Naming feelings** involves noticing the feelings, distinguishing between them, and accurately labeling them.

> **Understanding feelings** involves interpreting feelings, identifying cause and effect, and predicting how they will change.

You can see how both of these skills involve "thinking about feelings" as well as feeling them. Emotional literacy is a bridge between our emotions and our analysis. If the bridge is strong, we can do a great job interpreting feelings – if it's weak, we're probably coming to inept conclusions.

Some experts say emotional literacy also includes appropriately expressing feelings[1] – a skill Six Seconds puts into the competence of "Navigate Emotions." Emotional expression is a higher-level activity, a management task, so it's part of Choose Yourself. Still, it's a natural outgrowth of the first two, so often when I talk to parents and children about Emotional Literacy I include that component (just as children need to learn to use the right words to express a thought, they need to learn to appropriately express feelings).

*Our feelings
are our most genuine
paths to knowledge.*

— Audré Lorde

*For more on
Emotional Literacy,
see:*

www.6seconds.org/tag/emotions

&

www.6seconds.org/2011/07/26/integrated-emotions

Naming Feelings

One of the big obstacles to Emotional Literacy is a limited vocabulary. Walk down almost any street in America today and you'll hear people asking, "How are you?" The answer is almost invariably, "Oh, I'm fine. How about you?" "Well... I'm fine too, thanks for asking." "Fine" is NOT an emotion.

How many words do you know for feelings?

It helps to begin to categorize feelings. This lets us get started on recognizing and understanding them – as well as learning their names.

On the next page you'll see Figure 5.3, Feeling Log, whicg shows an adaptation of the Russell Circumplex Model (a model created for seeing how emotions are clustered in our language). There are two dimensions – how pleasant the feeling is, and how intense it is.

Challenge: Right now, I challenge you to take a large paper and draw that figure, and then put 30 feeling words in each quadrant.

This apparently simple process of developing a richer emotional vocabulary is a first step to mastering emotional intelligence.

Understanding Feelings

So looking at the Feeling Log (Figure 5.3), which quadrant is best? Is there one you'd like to be in all the time? That you'd like your employees in all the time?

Figure 5.3: Feeling Log

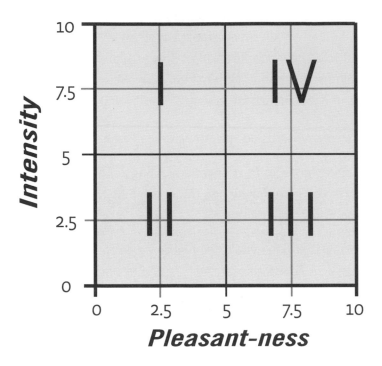

Feelings can be organized into these for quadrants; this helps provide a logical structure for understanding emotions.

- Quadrant 1 is intense, unpleasant feelings. Perhaps rage, grief, and disgust would go there.

- Quadrant 2 is mild, unpleasant feelings, such as boredom, irritation, or doubt.

- Quadrant 3 is for mild, pleasant feelings. Examples might be peacefulness, acceptance, or affection.

- Quadrant 4 contains intense, pleasant feelings. These might be ecstasy, adoration, triumph, or vigor.

Maybe you say, "II, because they will stay focused." True, but they won't confront big problems, they won't be innovative, and they won't work harder than necessary.

That's a problem. So maybe you want your employees in III all the time? In III they will be open and accepting, but again they won't confront problems, nor will they innovate.

Different situations call for different feelings. Each quadrant will affect thinking in different ways. At the most simple level, when our feelings are in quadrants I and II those feelings tell us, "Avoid this situation" (they signal danger or threat). Feelings in quadrants III and IV tell us, "Approach this!" These feelings signal safety and succor.

At a slightly more sophisticated level of interpretation, each quadrant causes us to notice different aspects of the environment.

Q	Feeling Words	Influence
I	Rage, Grief, Despair	Grapple with big problems
II	Discomfort, Annoyance	Focus on minor problems and issues
III	Calm, Peace, Caring	Foster openness and acceptance
IV	Delight, Triumph	Stimulate creativity and innovation

*It's surprising
how many persons
go through life
without ever recognizing
that their feelings
toward other people
are largely determined
by their feelings
toward themselves.*

Sydney J. Harris

Starting at a neurobiological level, feelings affect what we notice. Therefore, if we are not aware of our feelings and the effects of these feelings, our perceptions will be erroneous.

To further understand emotions, it may be useful to see how different emotions are related. As you learned in "Putting It In Practice" at the end of chapter four, every primary emotion can be more or less intense. To help you understand the progression of emotions, you can study the Plutchik Model (see Figure 5.4),[2] a flower-like depiction of the major emotions. Each petal of the flower shows a primary emotion – at the points you see a less intense variation; in the center a more intense one. The flower can "fold" into a cone. In the cone shape, you can see how as emotions become less intense, they actually become similar.

Imagine someone coming to work for you. He does not see the value of the work, it's not challenging or stimulating to him. So he experiences boredom. Weeks and months go by and nothing changes – he does not manage his feelings, and now he starts complaining about how bad this job is. He is feeling disgust. More time passes and the stimulae continue – the disgust will escalate into loathing, and he will start undermining, sabotaging, stealing, or he will just quit.

Now consider the opposite – literally the opposite, look on the other side of the model. That "petal" is trust. On the Plutchik Model, opposites are defined by the physiological

Figure 5.4: The Plutchik Model

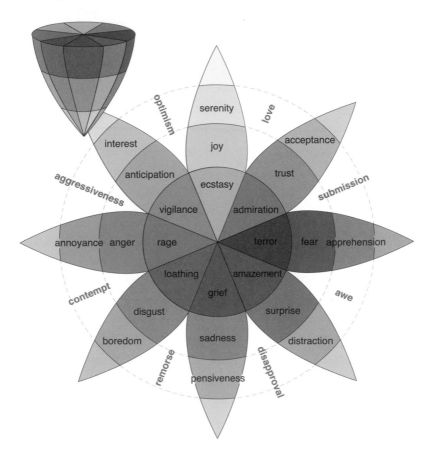

Plutchik's three-dimensional model (the cone) describes the relations among emotion concepts, which are analogous to the colors on a color wheel. The cone's vertical dimension represents intensity, and the circle represents degrees of similarity among the emotions. The eight sectors indicate that there are eight primary emotion dimensions; four pairs of opposites. In the exploded model (the larger graphic) the emotions in the blank spaces are the secondary feelings – mixtures of two of the primary emotions.

responses engendered by each emotion. The physiological response to disgust is to reject or push away; the opposite of that reaction is accept or embrace, and that's what trust motivates.

Imagine a different situation, the employee comes to work and he feels like people really welcome him, this is a place where he belongs. He feels acceptance. Over time, his voice is heard, and he has a sense of connection to the team – so he feels trust. As more time passes and the same stimuli continue, he will come to feel admiration and will be an advocate for the company both internally and externally.

The Plutchik Model also illustrates how emotions can combine into "secondary feelings." Only a few of the possible combinations are shown, but it gives you some examples. Secondary feelings are combinations of primary emotions. For example, when you feel both angry (ready to confront) and anticipation (looking for new data), you have a feeling called aggressiveness. When you feel joy (your preferences are met) and trust (connection and safety), the result is love.

The Angry Manager and The River

Anger is an emotion that is often misunderstood and blamed for all kinds of problems. There are two extremes when dealing with anger – venting and minimizing – and neither works. Anger's primary purpose is to alert people when their goals are being thwarted, which is helpful data. The anger causes attention to shift to the goal and can motivate action, but venting and minimizing both interfere with this function.

"Rick" is a manager who works in hospitality; he vents his anger. He is explosive; people are afraid of his temper. He throws the anger around – but paradoxically he doesn't acknowledge it. When you talk to him about his behavior he does not acknowledge the issue. "I'm just passionate," he says, "And I have really high standards."

"Cheryl" manages a professional services team; she minimizes her anger. Like Rick, she also struggles with anger, but people who work for her don't often know it. She's suppressing her feelings, and at the same time she is overly concerned about them. When I ask her about anger, she says "I'm overwhelmed with anger." When I ask why it's a problem, she says, "It's bad for me to be angry but I can't stop the feeling."

So here are two people experiencing fairly typical struggles with anger. The conventional response is, "See, anger is a bad feeling!" But what if that's wrong? What if anger is energy and information that neither Rick or Cheryl understands? They've both learned that "anger is bad," and they've internalized that belief.

Dr. William Evans, MD, works to help people find wholeness and health – integrating their physical, emotional, mental, and spiritual selves. He says that all of our bodily systems are healthier when they are flowing – our bodily systems (such as digestion, endocrine, blood, reproduction, immune) are all only able to function if they keep moving. In all the body's systems, blockages or overflows are symptoms or causes of illness; the same is almost certainly true of emotions.[3] In fact there is a whole emerging science studying "somatization," which is the physical internalizing of emotion (and the subsequent health risks).

Imagine a river. What happens if you take away the water, such as downstream from a dam? You get stagnation; it begins to stink, and the water literally becomes toxic. Cheryl is in this "drying" stage (and pretends she's not). Conversely, if you have too much water, you get a flood; the water goes beyond the banks and damages the land around it. Rick is in this "flood" stage (and pretends he's not).

The river is healthy when it is flowing. Just like emotions. Going to the extremes (ignoring them or over-emphasizing them, hiding from them or throwing them around, vilifying them or pretending they don't exist) doesn't work well. The challenge of emotional intelligence is to find the middle ground.

Restoring the Flow

The 123 KCG process can help Cheryl or Rick to turn their feelings into assets. Here is an example of how Rick could use the process:

> **Know**: Recognize anger. Notice it when it is getting started, when it's at a simmer, instead of waiting for it to be a full boil. Recognize the

EQ Competency:
Recognize Patterns

The human brain follows patterns, or neural pathways. Sets of ideas and feelings form that become our filters for how we interpret the world. Left unconscious, these patterns can inhibit optimal performance.

As a leader, Recognizing Patterns helps you predict your own reactions so you are not being driven by unconscious habits and reactions. Without this skill, leaders will be blind to the inner forces that drive their decisions and actions; they will be led by unconscious habits rather than leading from a position of clarity. Recognizing patterns is key to "mindfulness," that state of recognizing what's happening within.

pattern, the typical way you're responding, which is to vent the feeling.

Choose: Stop and evaluate the results of the pattern. Tune into the feeling of anger and understand it, recognize that it's trying to help you focus on an important issue; in this case probably an issue related to way you are communicating expectations to staff. Identify multiple options.

Give: What is most important for you in this situation? If your purpose is creating an exceptional experience for guests, what will move you toward that purpose? How can you enroll your team members in that purpose?

Recognize Patterns

Once people recognize their feelings, the next step is to see how they are reacting to the feeling. What are they doing in response?

For example, I was working with "Frank," a manager in a small financial services company. Frank was uncertain about how well he fit in at the company and was frequently doubting himself. He felt vulnerable, but he didn't like that feeling, so he covered it up by offering suggestions. He was constantly "solving" other people's problems so he could escape the feeling of vulnerability. It didn't work very well because people saw him as a meddler and micro-manager

Figure 5.5a: Wisdom of Feelings

Emotion: *Joy*

Purpose/Signal: Achieving Goals; Expanding Possibilities

A Time I Felt This...

What was the **wisdom of the feeling?**

Emotion: *Fear*

Purpose/Signal: Uncertainty; Uknown Danger; Powerlessness

A Time I Felt This...

What was the **wisdom of the feeling?**

Emotion: *Anger*

Purpose/Signal: Road is Blocked; Change Needed

A Time I Felt This...

What was the **wisdom of the feeling?**

Fill in this chart (here and on next pages) to help clarify your understanding of emotions. See "Cause and Effect" on page 129.

instead of an ally. His pattern was, "when I feel vulnerable, I fix." Recognizing this he was able to change it.

Learning to observe a reaction in process is critical for understanding our emotional drivers. We all follow patterns of reaction; when we think or feel a certain way, we respond unconsciously with a particular set of thoughts, feelings, and actions. When I feel threatened, I attack. When I think someone is judging my ideas, I feel defensive.

The "Recognize Patterns" competency allows us to observe this process in action. Coupled with Emotional Literacy, our own reactions and their emotional drivers become clear. Learning to observe and understand ourselves also gives us insight into what's driving others and our part in that.

If we don't recognize the pattern it will be next to impossible to change it (in Choose Yourself). Even more urgently, if we don't know our own patterns of reaction, we can undermine our own goals and influence others in destructive ways – without even noticing.

To begin Recognizing Patterns it's important to observe yourself (or others) without judgment. This means avoiding coming to a conclusion of what's "good" or "bad." To develop skill at Recognizing Patterns, it is helpful be like a scientist observing (that's why our school curriculum is called "Self-Science"). Notice your behaviors and the situations that recur in your life. Then notice the feelings and thoughts that

Figure 5.5b: Wisdom of Feelings

Emotion: **Sadness**

Purpose/Signal: Not Achieving Goals; Something Important is Missing; Loss of Love

A Time I Felt This...

What was the **wisdom of the feeling?**

Emotion: **Acceptance**

Purpose/Signal: Recognize Value; Openness

A Time I Felt This...

What was the **wisdom of the feeling?**

Emotion: **Anticipation**

Purpose/Signal: Planning Ahead; Seeking New Situation

A Time I Felt This...

What was the **wisdom of the feeling?**

are attached. Name the pattern using this formula: "When _(stimulus)_ , I _(typical response)_ ." Keep observing and refining until you can be very specific.

Cause and Effect

To practice emotional literacy and synthesize the ideas in this chapter, I invite you to try this exercise. Every feeling has value – not always apparent – that can be accessed if you can "listen" to the feeling carefully. The challenge is to see the wisdom in the feeling that may be obscured by assumptions, mixed feelings, or being in a rush. The premise is that each feeling is a message (from you to you), and each emotion has a specific purpose – it signals something essential (such as a core value, or a risk, or an important opportunity).

I've listed several emotions in Figures 5.5 A, B, and C and given possible purposes. Remember a time when you had each feeling, note it down, and see if you can feel that feeling again. While you are feeling it, reflect on what you've learned about emotional literacy, and see if you can find the wisdom in each one – what is the value, the life-saving message, the core principle being reinforced, or the subtle insight?

Caveat

While we can use theoretical models to explore emotions, feelings are fundamentally subjective. Feeling is, by

Figure 5.5c: Wisdom of Feelings

Emotion: **Disgust**

Purpose/Signal: Something is Unacceptable; Reject or Move Away

A Time I Felt This...

What was the **wisdom of the feeling?**

Emotion: **Surprise**

Purpose/Signal: Reality is Different Than Beliefs; Re-evaluate

A Time I Felt This...

What was the **wisdom of the feeling?**

definition, a non-analytic experience. We put these models and maps together to help make sense of and communicate about this incredibly complex subject. The models are helpful, and they are not "The Truth." My intention in sharing them is to provide a framework for reflection.

Don't over-analyze, don't try to turn emotions into formulae. Instead, use the models as a diver uses SCUBA gear – make them tools for helping you explore the hidden mysteries of the iceberg.

Chapter Five Notes

1   Emotional Literacy: My friend and colleague Ayman Sawaf created the Foundation for Education in Emotional Literacy (FEEL) in 1983. He is the co-author of *Executive EQ*, and the producer of 2 movies, a children's show, and 21 children's books on the subject (see www.KidsEQ.com).

2   Plutchik Model: This graphic representation of the basic emotions appeared in Plutchik, Robert (2001). "The Nature of Emotions," *American Scientist*, July-August 2001. Figure reprinted by permission of *American Scientist*, magazine of Sigma Xi, The Scientific Research Society.

3   Evans, William M.D., personal correspondence May 2006. Dr. Evans studies optimal human function and the link between physical, mental, emotional, and spiritual wellness in contemporary society.

Chapter Five Recap

Key Concept:

Emotions contain data about what's happening inside us and with others; we can learn to accurately interpret that data. Emotions affect our perceptions.

Related Reading:

Emotional Equations, **Chip Conley**

Emotions Revealed, **Paul Ekman**

The Emotionally Intelligent Manager, **David Caruso and Peter Salovey**

Key Practice:

BMH Scan: Take about six seconds to "scan" (notice) each of these three areas:

B: Body – physical sensations. Where are you tight, sore, hot, cold, etc. This gives you clues about your current state and puts your attention in the present.

M: Mind – cognitive activity. What are you thinking about, where is your attention focused (problems, solutions, issues, opportunities, etc)? This gives you information about how your feelings are influencing you and increases your clarity.

H: Heart – feelings. What are the 3-5 different feelings you have in this moment? This increases your emotional literacy and helps you develop self-awareness.

Chapter Six

Choose Yourself:
Fight or Flow

You are the instrument of leadership. The way you show up each day, the way you react, the way you live, these are the tools you have for inspiring others to be and do their best. Once you see how emotions affect performance, and you want to manage those powerful drivers, your most powerful tool is your own emotion. Emotions are contagious: Others will pick up on your feelings and their emotions will change.[1] Moreover, these "transmitted" feelings change the way people solve problems, interact with each other and customers, and either increase or decrease efficacy.

What emotional messages are you spreading? Do those help you achieve your vision and mission?

I was in Singapore eating one of my favorite Chinese delicacies, a dumpling called "xiao long bao" which is a rare treat for me – we don't have a lot of these on the Central Coast of California! They looked delicious, steaming, juicy, and succulent. I picked up the first one, but just then I

Be Strategic with Emotions:

*What do you want to feel,
and what do you want
others to feel?*

- David Caruso[2]

started thinking about a problem with one of our products that's behind schedule. I chewed and hardly noticed the taste of the dumpling. Then I was kind of disappointed, wondering "what's wrong with me that I can't just enjoy a peaceful lunch and leave work at work?" So as I ate the second one I was paying attention, but I was not enjoying it because of my feelings of scarcity and judgment. I decided to change my mood, and to really appreciate the flavor of the third one. It was absolutely delicious!

Even in something so simple I had choice about the way I live. By changing my feelings and the direction of my attention, I could experience the moment in a dramatically different way. At that lunch it was so clear to me that I could choose to be distracted and reactive or mindful and intentional; it just takes a heartbeat to shift. I suggest you try this at lunch today! This is the point of "Choosing Yourself" — it's about intentionally living your life as someone who is awake, present, and clear — and having that kind of effect on others.

As a leader I can walk into a situation in the absent-minded way of the first dumpling and I miss what's important. I can be in the stress reaction of the second dumpling and influence those around me to be negative and frustrated; this is so common in our world today with the pressure and scarcity we often face. Or, through a simple shift of attention and feeling, I can be awake enough to make good decisions and to influence others effectively — and enjoy the process.

Figure 6.1: The Escalator

Each time we go around the reaction cycle, we move further up the escalator — and the more volatile we are. Up the escalator we tend to react more quickly, and also more defensively (with one of the three Fs: Fight, Flee, Freeze).

If we are going to be intelligent with our emotions, we can start to use them strategically. This means planning ahead to develop and elicit the optimal emotions for different situations. We begin to choose our own emotions and to create an optimal performance state. Perhaps it is possible to do this in a superficial and manipulative way, but I believe the only sustainable method is to genuinely transform our own emotions so they, in turn, can influence others. In the Six Seconds Model this is called "Navigate Emotions."

The Choose Yourself part of the Six Seconds Model focuses on four key competencies that allow us to assess our choices and shift to new emotions and behaviors – driven from the inside. "Fight or Flow" explores how, when we know ourselves, we can begin to do that transformation so we can show up as we intend.

This is absolutely critical from a leadership perspective. If we're going to lead, we need to be stepping out in front creating ripples that pull others along. If we're in reaction, in the fight, people will not follow us.

Up the Escalator: The Reaction Cycle

Think of an escalator. When you are in your calm, balanced state – flow – you're near the bottom of the escalator. In this state it's easy to handle adversity and challenge with a kind of effortless grace that is truly inspiring.

Figure 6.2: Reaction Cycle

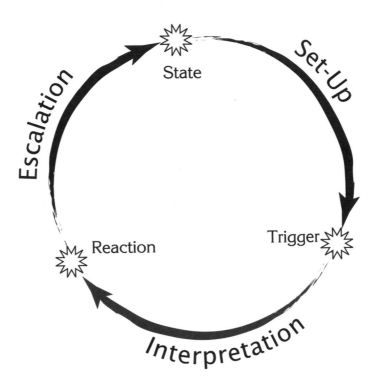

When we experience a reaction (fight, flight, or freeze) it is not an isolated event. Instead, the reaction is a cycle starting with a set-up (such as being in a hurry), then a trigger (such as someone driving poorly). We then interpret that stimulus, react, and then, if we're staying in reaction, we escalate. This leads to a heightened state, which becomes a set-up for the next time around.

If, however, you've had frustration and stress building up, not sleeping enough, eating poorly, avoiding exercising, not nurturing your spiritual self, thinking about all the problems... pretty soon you start climbing the reaction escalator.

Each step you take up the escalator follows the cycle of reaction. There are three phases: Set-Up, Interpretation, and Escalation (see Figure 6.2).

In the **Set-Up** stage you are moving toward reactivity. You are setting yourself up for a fall. For example, you might be cutting short your sleep, eating unhealthy foods, overworking, and focusing on problems – this will cause a physical, emotional, and mental state prone to reaction.

Then something happens – a trigger. Maybe someone argues with you, or you see a negative interaction, or you just have a thought that is frustrating, stressful, or upsetting.

Next you **Interpret**. You perceive the trigger as a threat, a danger, a problem, etc. It's a very quick process – just ¼ of a second. Part of your brain called the thalamus is responsible for this process – it's like a regulation valve for the flow of sensory information and it's highly attuned to threat. When the thalamus perceives the threat, it triggers your Autonomic Nervous System (ANS) and causes a chain reaction to occur releasing a flood of chemicals.

As the reaction proceeds, you might now **Escalate** – taking another step up the escalator. Your thoughts and feelings are interacting to reinforce the flood of chemicals. Your Autonomic Nervous System activates your Sympathetic Nervous System preparing you to fight, flee, or freeze. Floods of adrenaline are released to power your muscles. Cortisol is released to maintain the high alert. You probably think about how bad and awful the other person in the situation is, and how right and virtuous you are, fueling this cycle with your judgment.

It is a cycle, so the Escalation becomes Set-Up for the next time around the circle. Each time you go around, you step up the escalator, raising the internal threat level, setting the "danger radar" to a more and more sensitive setting. The first few times around the cycle it may be invisible to others – you are reacting internally, setting the stage for further reaction. But each time around you are coming closer and closer to an explosion.

"Hit Back First"

Have you ever seen one of those fountains where a large stone sphere seems to float on a cushion of water? Hundreds of pounds of rock glide in swirling circles – apparently effortless.

What if we could interact with other people with that same calm, powerful, effortless ease? What if our leadership could flow in that kind of smoothness – like the calmly focused

sea captain who keeps the crew safe and triumphant through his very presence at the helm despite the fury of the raging storm.

When we get caught up in small tensions and conflicts it's challenging to stay in "flow." Minor issues escalate because both sides "need to be right" as a defense mechanism. Why does it happen?

At the very core of our being is a set of reactions that help us survive. Thousands of years of practice have refined our ability to protect ourselves from threat and danger. We don't have turtle-like shells or tiger-like fangs – we have super-sensitive brains.

When our brains perceive a threat, they react to protect us; it's a survival response built into the limbic brain (or "emotional brain"). Depending on biology and experience, that protection comes from fighting, fleeing, or freezing. Some people also add another "f" – "flocking" or herding together. It is almost impossible to avoid that impulse, we are literally hard-wired to react that way to defend against threat.

So, if I threaten you, I can almost guarantee that you will react by fighting, fleeing, or freezing. You will "be defensive" by attacking back, retreating, evading, or ganging up with others. Of course, depending on the intensity of your reaction, you can almost guarantee that I will respond with one of those as well.

The "threat response" is part of what Dr. Daniel Goleman called "hijacking the amygdala" and is well defined in Dr. Joseph LeDoux's research.[3] The amygdala is one of the

We want the facts
to fit the preconceptions.

When they don't, it is easier
to ignore the facts
than to change
the preconceptions.

— Jessamyn West

primary emotional centers in the brain; one core function is reacting to perceived danger. As Dr. Peter Salovey explains, this reaction is actually an example of the intelligence of our emotions – a kind of "emotional logic" is followed and decisions are made with little or no cognitive thought; the problem is that few of us have developed this aspect of our intelligence.[4]

So what constitutes "threat" from the amygdala's point of view? Almost any interaction where someone is trying to take power over someone else will trigger the "survival response." People try to take power by putting others down, shaming, blaming, embarrassing, judging, discrediting, and dividing.

This dynamic plays out all the time in many offices. One person feels threatened or vulnerable, so they come in with bluster and anger as a defense. It happens constantly in families and schools too. I want to be right so I walk in blaming and judging, putting down other people; if I "make them less" it seems to strengthen my position.

When I attack, I can almost guarantee that the other person will react in survival mode, and the situation will escalate. I might think I am being tactful, but if I am feeling hurt or angry, it comes out. It happens almost every time. Yet, time after time, I see myself and others surprised and disappointed when people are defensive!

Perhaps the surprise comes because most of us believe we have a good "poker face," a mask that will hide our real feelings. "I can be hurt, frustrated, and impatient," I think to myself, "but I'll 'put that aside' and ask you calmly what happened." Guess what? I "calmly" ask you what happened, and you react like I've said, "You screwed up and I'm hurt, frustrated, and impatient!"

Think how often something like this happens to you: Even though you're totally annoyed, you try and "put aside your feelings" and act calmly... but despite that effort people **still** respond as if you've attacked them.

Another survival mechanism in our limbic brains causes this interaction. Not only do we act to protect when attacked, we are keenly sensitive to potential threats. The limbic brain actually seeks out feelings in others that indicate danger – it's like a "Danger Radar." A danger radar looking for potentially hostile emotions, such as anger, frustration, fear, anxiety, rejection, and disgust. Anxiety is a major issue in today's stressful environment – our brains are constantly alerting us to be prepared for battle.

When you and I are talking, the danger radar in your limbic brain is checking me out. Let's say I am trying to appear calm, but underneath I'm really frustrated. Not with you, I'm just frustrated about something I heard on the phone. So I talk to you, and ask you to work on a project. My words are not unreasonable, but underneath your radar is picking something up. You're sensing that my words and my feelings don't match (because you are noticing, perhaps unconsciously, thousands of small cues from body language and facial expression). You might not know exactly what I'm feeling, you simply sense there's an issue. Just the mismatch itself is enough to create fear in you – after all, I'm hiding something from you, and you're limbic brain knows that when people are deceiving you, it might be because they want to hurt you.

One way our "danger radar" works is by reading facial expressions and tone of voice. In Dr. Albert Mehrabian's research at UCLA, the team found that only 7% of the emotional content of communication comes in words – the rest is tone, body language, and expression.[5] Dr. Paul Ekman's work on facial expression reinforces this conclusion; Ekman has found people display a massive amount of emotional information through "microexpressions" that flit across all our faces. While most people notice general patterns of these expressions, Ekman says, very few can accurately "read" a stream of micro expressions.[6] So, while we can tell in general that someone is vexed and trying to hide it, we probably can't tell if their displeasure is directed at us!

In any case, in the midst of our interaction, there is a lot of room for the underlying emotions and intentions to influence thinking. You might not know exactly what's going on with me, but you sense a lack of congruence or authenticity. Depending on your feelings and experience, and our relationship, your limbic brain sends you to battle stations, and we can become reactive to one another very quickly.

Given this dynamic, it's no wonder people spend so much time and energy attacking and defending, being right, making others wrong. "Flowing" like the stone ball fountain is tremendously challenging amidst all this hostility.

EQ Competency:
Apply Consequential Thinking

This skill lets us pause to examine the consequences of our choices – preferably before we act! It is key to managing our impulses and acting intentionally (rather than reacting).

As a leader, Applying Consequential Thinking will help you plan mindfully and act intentionally, assessing your options and choosing the ones that provide optimal results. Once the plan is in place, this competence helps leaders stay on course and maintain focus. Leaders who do not have this skill are likely impulsive, reactive, and surprised by the results they get. This can cause others to see them as volatile and less trustworthy.

In the Six Seconds Model, being aware of and managing this cycle is called "Consequential Thinking." It's a competency in feeling and thinking ahead and assessing so we can choose the most effective alternative. It's different than strategic planning because it takes emotions into account as a source of essential information about the world inside and outside of us.

Applying Consequential Thinking requires us to take into account our feelings as well as our analysis as we consider our actions. To weigh the costs and benefits of our choices – both in terms of the rational side "above the surface" of the iceberg, and the unintended consequences affecting the hidden 10/11^{ths}. When we Apply Consequential Thinking, we are monitoring the impulse to "Hit Back First."

Some tips:

1. People defend themselves (with one of the Fs) when they perceive danger.

2. Our brains are on the lookout for emotions that could signal danger, such as anger, fear, or distrust. A mismatch between words, expression, and feelings is a danger signal (it arouses mistrust).

3. Greater anxiety and/or stress increases the "danger alert level" so we're even more sensitive and vigilant.

4. If there is any "attack" in our approach, we invite – almost guarantee – a defense. Even if we try to hide our frustration and anger it provokes a reaction.

I have found that many people – myself included – don't particularly like to look at the "Hit Back First" parts of ourselves. It takes a real sense of safety to explore this. By definition you don't feel safe when your danger radar is buzzing, so it's quite a challenge. You may find yourself avoiding this investigation by being defensive, trivializing, or even hitting yourself back (e.g., self-criticizing or demeaning yourself).

If you find yourself avoiding looking at your patterns around reactivity, it may be because you're also making judgments about what you observe (ie., telling yourself that something is wrong or right, that it should be one way not another, or even that this is an exception not the rule). Notice the judgments (don't judge yourself for having them), and tell yourself, "Yes, that's one possible judgment (and there are other reasonable conclusions too)."

While you're struggling for primacy in the fight, you will always have to strive. When you choose to practice your emotional wisdom, to practice living in flow, you will discover a true strength that liberates you from the need to show how powerful you are.

"Water Is Stronger"

It's always amazed me that these heavy stones in the fountains can move – float – on a cushion of water. The water is so calm, yet so powerful. It's not powerful because it's loud, fast, or fierce: the effectiveness comes from the consistency and the balance.

I've been told that in feng-shui the water represents "movement, money, and/or emotion." The ball can represent the self, symbolizing that we can sink or float in our emotions.

The challenge, for me, is to discover the effortlessness – the opposite of "Hitting Back First." Some people call it surrender, some call is peace, some call it "the zone"; I like the word "acceptance." How, in the midst of the stress of daily life, do I use my emotion as a source of power and effortlessly float like the stone?

This attitude begins with the recognition that we have a choice. In the Six Seconds Model, the second key pursuit of EQ is called "Choose Yourself." *Choose Yourself* means taking ownership for your own results, taking back your life, and acting as you intend. There are four key competencies that make it possible:

1. Apply Consequential Thinking lets you evaluate the choices you're making – ideally before you act (rather than reacting without regard to the costs and benefits).

2. Navigate Emotions gives you the insight from feelings and lets you transform them into a source of information and energy (rather than a source of confusion and struggle).

3. Exercise Optimism provides you with options so you can have multiple choices from which to choose (as opposed to being a victim without any choice).

Figure 6.3: A Floating Stone

The Millennium Ball fountain in Amarillo, Texas. The ball weighs over 3,000 pounds and can be spun with a child's touch.

4. Engage Intrinsic Motivation delivers fuel to make the changes based on your internal commitments (rather than being blown with the wind).

Applying these four competencies results in a kind of self-mastery where you can respond rather than react, where you are following your intentions rather than your hot buttons. First, let's revisit the strife. I'll use myself as an example, but you might be very different; what's challenging for me might be easy for you – so think about what's challenging for you. When it's easy, it's easy! It's the challenges that require a stretch.

In "Hit Back First!" I suggested you invest time becoming more aware of your own Danger Radar. My Danger Radar, and perhaps many people's, is particularly sensitive to my fear of losing power. If I feel a sense of helplessness, of fear, or loss of control, I am very uncomfortable, and my inclination is to grab for some power.

In those moments of disequilibrium, I feel compelled to show (myself, mostly) that I am not helpless, incompetent, or weak. I try to exert power over another by being right, or by showing I have the answer, or by dismissing another's point of view and demonstrating my expertise. It could be being "more right than" colleagues, employees, my boss, my children, my spouse, my mother, etc. Notice that I try to exert power OVER them, which means that in addition to being right and smart, I have to be more right, smarter, better – and that means they have to be less. We're back to a battle between limbic systems.

EQ Competency:
Navigate Emotions

People are often told to control their emotions, to suppress feelings like anger, joy, or fear, and cut them off from the decision making process. But feelings provide insight, energy, and are the real basis for almost every decision.

As a leader, Navigating Emotions helps you tap the energy and information in feelings to find the wisdom. It is essential for self-management and personal mastery – which comes across as authentic strength. Together with emotional literacy it is the key to the "inner knowing" often called "gut feel" or "intuition." People without this skill get stuck in certain feelings or are overwhelmed by feelings so they distance themselves from emotion and are seen as either cold or volatile.

In this situation, there is an interaction between my thoughts and feelings, and I am choosing both. Sometimes emotion comes first, sometimes thought, and there is a constant, fluid exchange. Being aware of the play between emotion and thought is one key to practicing emotional intelligence. It is complicated because in the escalation, there is not a single transaction calculated by one belief, but a system, a flow, of thoughts, feelings, and actions influencing one another.

And, because the limbic system actively looks for input from other people, I am also strongly influenced by the thoughts, feelings, and actions of people around me. That doesn't mean I am a victim of another person's whim, it does mean we are interconnected and we affect one another.

Our society has minimized, trivialized, and even vilified emotions to the point where many people won't even admit to having them. We even call cognitive thought "high order thinking" because scientists once "knew" that rational processes were more "advanced" than confusing emotions. Thankfully, the last decade has seen a sea-change, and more and more people are reassessing their feelings about feelings and seeing their value.

The first step is recognizing, "If I don't deal with feelings, they will cause me problems." The second is, "Feelings are valuable in and of themselves." In *The Feeling of What Happens*,[7] Antonio Damasio goes a step further to say that our very consciousness – our awareness of our own thoughts, is created by emotion. In an interview, Damasio

In the long run,
we shape our lives
and we shape ourselves.

The process never
ends until we die,

and the choices
that we make
are ultimately
our responsibility.

— Eleanor Roosevelt

told me "your life is like a movie, and your consciousness is how you know you're watching the movie. It's your feelings that create the awareness of your life." He says without emotion we'd actually lose all perspective of what's important and our role in the continuity of our lives.

In any case, most of us grew up "knowing" that feelings were in the way of clear thinking, and we learned to put them aside. It makes the work of listening to them somewhat more challenging. To do so, we need to develop competency at Navigating Emotions. It's not "controlling" feelings, rather it's listening to, understanding, and transforming them.

In Navigating Emotions, the goal is a partnership – an alliance – between the rational and emotional. Like the water and the stone in the fountain. Without the water, the stone is stuck; without the stone, the water is just a pool.

I've found it helpful to remember these two lessons from the stone-ball fountains:

1. The water is powerful, and the power comes from gentle persistence.

2. Sometimes the system gets stuck and can get unstuck.

The Powerful Water: Navigating Emotions

It's important to understand what makes the water powerful. When the fountain is in balance, the water is persistent, constantly flowing... it is smooth, putting pressure evenly on the stone... it is moving and changing... it is gentle, not spraying all over.

If I have choice about my feelings, then I can choose to experience my emotion in those balanced ways. For myself, simply accepting that I **can** experience emotion that way is a big step to actually having it happen. It helps me to see the polarities of my choice so that while I am in the moment, I can know what I'm choosing. Here are three dimensions of choice:

1. I can let emotion flow and change, or I can be stuck in one emotion, constantly re-creating the same feelings.

2. I can experience emotion in a smooth constancy, or I can try to force it aside (until it pops out).

3. I can let emotion flow gently, or I can use it like a cudgel to beat on other people.

You don't have to wait for some "big moment" to look at the way you're experiencing emotions. You can take the opportunity right now – below is a chart with the three dimensions of choice – where are you on each axis right now?

Fluid	vs	Stuck
Feel	vs	Suppress
Gentle	vs	Forceful

Tuning into the way you experience and use emotion (reflecting on the three dimensions above) will help you become more effective with your feelings. Just as you learned about your "Danger Radar," give yourself time to focus and observe how your other emotions function.

Caution: Resistance Ahead

As you explore the ways you're experiencing and using emotion, you may find you resist approaching or actually feeling some feelings. You may have learned that they are wrong or bad or dangerous — I'm not saying they really are wrong, bad, or dangerous, but we've all had experiences that may have pushed us to believe that (such as having a terrible conflict tied to a certain feeling, or being blamed for feeling a particular way).

It's very hard to experience feelings that we suspect to be unsafe. Your emotional brain is all about safety, so it will resist when you engage in "unsafe feeling." Let's say you've had unpleasant experiences with sorrow and so you associate that feeling with risk and adversity. At some level you "know" sorrow is dangerous so you avoid it. Then after reading this book and the three dimensions of choice, you decide to let yourself feel sad. You may find yourself doing almost anything but! You might start trying to feel this feeling, but it's elusive.

People are incredibly good at resisting — we undermine, side track, attack, retreat... it's like pushing your finger down

EQ Competency:
Engage Intrinsic Motivation

If we require external reinforcement to be motivated, we are always at the mercy of others. This skill galvanizes us to discover and engage the lasting inner motivation that lets us make change and grow.

As a leader, Engaging Intrinsic Motivation helps you gain the energy to do the hard work, and be true to your own vision rather than being unduly influenced by others. Leaders without this skill seek approval from others and come across as weak or passive. High scores on Intrinsic Motivation also predict a significant portion of personal effectiveness.

firmly on an oily cutting board – you keep slipping around the point you were trying to touch. Or, as our Southern friends might say, "It's like wrestling with a greased pig." If you're experimenting with letting yourself feel emotions, one likely way of resisting is questioning the validity of the whole exercise (you may hear yourself thinking, "this is stupid, I should just put these feelings aside and get back to work!" – maybe true, maybe not – but most likely it's the voice of your own resistance). So you won't get past this point if you don't notice your own resistance, recommit to your goal, and persevere.

This is why the competency of Intrinsic Motivation is so important to Choose Yourself. Intrinsic Motivation drives you to persevere despite the discomfort or embarrassment. It requires you shift your attention from "What will others think?" to "What is right for me." You probably have developed considerable Intrinsic Motivation if you are in a leadership role or have worked hard to reach this point in your life and career. Perhaps the next challenge is looking carefully at how you engender that in others – how you create real independence and interdependence versus holding tight to power and control.

It's important to see that as long as you are holding onto control, you are keeping others from being fully accountable for their own choices. They can simply blame you for whatever happens. The more you take charge of others, the less they have to take charge of themselves. At the same time, you are setting yourself up to be stuck in power-struggle of battling egos.

As a leader there is an incredible challenge here. People look to you for answers and direction – and you may know a better way. But when you take over you are creating dependence. So look at your workplace relationships and the way you interact: Are you asking people to be obedient, or are you fostering internal motivation?

Tuning the Intelligence

Recently I asked an eminent psychologist if he would announce one of our conferences to his mailing list. He wrote me, "Everyone knows that feelings are irrational and undermining of logical analysis, so this whole idea of 'emotional intelligence' is an oxymoron." Upon reflection, here's my answer: Have you ever made a mistake doing math? Does that mean mathematical intelligence is an oxymoron?

We all have emotional intelligence, but that doesn't mean all our emotions are intelligent! I certainly have had many experiences where I've been overwhelmed by feelings, or overly reactive, or just plain confused. So every feeling may not be useful in every moment, and not all people are adept at knowing the difference. Our job is to refine this intelligence. Just as we learned algebra and figured out how to "solve for x," we can choose to learn to successfully solve the emotional equations in our lives.

The intelligence of emotions comes because these feelings provide information and "weight" to influence decision making. Feelings give us a subtle insight – information about what's going on inside us, and with others. You can block that information by resisting the feelings – by suppressing them. You can also lose the information by going to the opposite extreme and using feeling as a cudgel or wallowing in them. In either case, you're trying to manipulate the feelings rather than listening to yourself. By practicing letting your emotions flow gently, you will begin to gain insight from that subtle emotional awareness.

When I get stuck and sucked into the patterns of strife, the situation always seems deadly serious – like some core belief or need is being threatened. Suddenly I am on high alert, ready to do battle.

Then I think of those fountains and remember that I have a simple choice: fight or flow.

Both have costs and benefits, both have challenges and opportunities. If I choose flow, though, suddenly the strife seems a bit silly – perhaps important, but certainly not deadly serious.

Practicing living like the stone-ball fountain is a lifelong process of letting go of primal fears. These fears are tied to the extrinsic – to other people's perceptions and judgments. When you really build your Intrinsic Motivation these forces will diminish. Still, you've had a lifetime to learn to protect yourself by using emotions a certain way. Recognize it will take time to change the way you relate to your emotions.

As human beings,
our greatness lies
not so much in being able
to remake the world
— that is the myth
of the atomic age —
as in being able
to remake ourselves.

— Mahatma Gandhi

Here are a few key steps:

- Let go the belief that flowing is weak – look at mighty mountains carved by streams.

- Let go the fear that emotions will overwhelm you if you actually feel them – look at the stone floating smoothly.

- Let go the terror of being different – look at the glorious rainbow of an ocean reef and all the variety that makes it so delightful.

- Let go your hurry to know it now – look how long it's taking to find a cure for the common cold.

- Let go the embarrassment of being wrong – look at the stunning risks that have advanced science, taken by people like Galileo, Da Vinci, Marconi, Curie, Edison who did what everyone "knew" was impossible.

At the core, remember your emotions are seeking your safety. When you have a strong reaction, know that it's a message that some part of you feels unsafe. When someone else has a strong reaction, know that she or he feels unsafe. Don't trivialize that reaction, recognize it as valid and valuable. Then help both of you find the courage to persevere past the fear – to gracefully flow into the risk of learning and growing. Use the pressure of the emotions to successfully float the stone ball.

EQ Competency:
Exercise Optimism

Optimism allows us to see beyond the present and take ownership of the future. This skill blends thinking and feeling to shift our beliefs and attitudes to a more proactive stance.

As a leader, Exercising Optimism lets you find innovative solutions and it energizes you and others. Pessimistic leaders foster distrust and self-protection; they are less inspiring and less innovative. In addition, our research shows high Optimism scores predict good health.

Down the Escalator: Optimism and Renewal

As I said earlier, the "top of the escalator" crisis is not a singular transaction, but rather part of a sequence; each time around the reaction cycle the pressure builds up. Then, when I have a major reaction and fight, flee, or freeze, it's because I've set myself up. I've made choices that sent me up the escalator.

High up the escalator, a small issue turns into an explosion. I'm vulnerable. I'm reactive. And I am not effective as a leader because instead of articulating and modeling a vision, I'm defending, fighting, and hiding. I'm in distress. How often does this happen to you?

Many business people (maybe even most) have spent so long near the top of the escalator they don't even recognize that their "baseline" stress level is near the boiling point. They don't remember what it is like down at the bottom of the escalator – in fact, they think "I'm relaxed" when they're ¾ of the way up the escalator! Whole organizations form patterns around this high stress – and people make bad decisions, there is no accountability, communication suffers, and the organization flails.

As Richard Boyatzis and Annie McKee discuss in *Resonant Leadership*,[8] it is imperative that leaders build in a practice of renewal – that they get down from the escalator on a regular basis. If you Know Yourself, you will recognize when you're up the escalator. Part of Choosing Yourself is taking care of yourself so that you can face each day at your very best.

Figure 6.4: The Optimism Difference

Someone using an optimistic style will explain their success or failure in a specific manner. There are three elements to consider: [9]

Time / Duration:

Permanent   ...   Temporary

Isolation / Scope

Pervasive   ...   Isolated

Effort / Personal Involvement

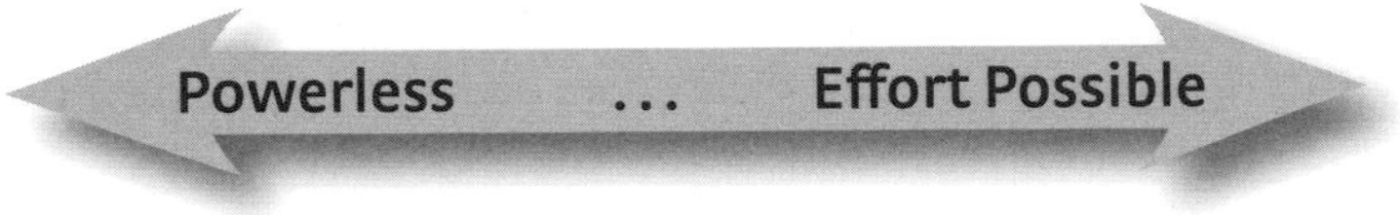

Powerless   ...   Effort Possible

The pessimistic voice says a failure or problem is Permanent, Pervasive, and Powerless (PPP) - and a success or achievement is Temporary, Isolated, and Effort not involved (TIE).

The optimistic voice says a failure or problem is Temporary, Isolated, and Effort is possible (TIE) – while success is Permanent, Pervasive, and due to personal Power (PPP).

The Six Seconds Model assists with Renewal. By recognizing feelings, identifying options, and connecting to your Noble Goal, you will move down the escalator and restore your vitality. It becomes automatic.

If you are going to pick just one competency in the model, though, Exercising Optimism is essential to renewal because it shifts you out of the downward spiral. One reason we get stressed, perhaps the only reason, is that we come to see we're powerless. Burnout may be due more to a perceived lack of choice than overwork. We have a problem that we don't see that we can solve, we feel stuck. So we begin a cycle of pessimistic thinking.

Every one of us has times when we use an optimistic style, and times we use a pessimistic style. The pessimistic interpretation causes problems to seem bigger; even insurmountable.

Dr. Martin Seligman is a psychologist who studied mental illness for several decades, and then came to see that curing illness was not enough: Psychologists also need to help individuals create happiness. His extensive research on optimism shows that an optimistic style can be learned – and that optimists live longer, are more successful, healthier, and have better marriages.[9]

The secret of optimism is challenging the voices in your head that say, "This will never get better." "This is ruining everything." And, "There is nothing I can do." Instead, practice the approach that problems are temporary (they will pass), isolated (they don't affect everything), and that effort will make a difference (you have not tried everything yet). It helps to look at these three dimensions and see the poles (see Figure 6.4).

When you consider a success or failure, an achievement or a setback, listen to the words you use (out loud and in your own head). How are you explaining this situation? Are you using the voice of optimism? If not, challenge yourself to explain it another way.

In our research using the Six Seconds Emotional Intelligence test, optimism is an important component of leadership – and alone it predicts 20.5% of the variation in health scores.[10] Since health includes both physical vigor and stress management, you can see why optimism is essential to maintaining your focus and power as a leader.

Chapter Six Recap

Key Concept:

We have a choice about our reactions. It begins by noticing the warning signs that we are out of balance and restoring our equilibrium.

Related Reading:

Resonant Leadership, Richard Boyatzis and Annie McKee[11]

Learned Optimism, Martin Seligman[12]

Key Practice:

Navigate Emotions: Rather than "controlling" feelings at a surface level, engage with them. Let yourself feel the emotion, listen to it, explore it, and let it change. This requires several additional competencies discussed in the chapter.

Chapter Six Notes

1   "Infectious" or "Contagious" emotions is a "hot topic" in research right now. We have a White Paper on this on 6seconds.org showing that one person's emotions change another person's, and the resultant feelings affect performance. Sigal Barsade is doing a great deal of research on this subject, for example see Barsade, S.G. (2002). The Ripple Effect: Emotional Contagion and its Influence on Group Behavior. *Administrative Science Quarterly,* 47 (4), 644-675

2   David Caruso works with John Mayer and Peter Salovey, the pioneering scientists who showed that there is such a thing as emotional intelligence. They made a test that measures this "basic level" process of thinking and feeling working together, it is called the MSCEIT. David's been a great ally to me and helped me understand how emotions and thinking really can work together – I highly recommend taking the MSCEIT when you are ready to explore the core concepts of emotional intelligence (www.EQstore. com). It's somewhat abstract, so maybe better after you've worked on the subject for awhile.

3   Hijacking: See LeDoux, JE (1994) "Emotion, Memory, and the Brain" *Scientific American* – or his web site: http://www.cns.nyu.edu/home/ledoux/

4   Dr. Salovey shared this perspective with me in a personal conversation at NexusEQ South Africa in 2001

5   Nonverbal communication: studies by Albert Mehrabian in the 1970s at UCLA found that when communicating about preferences, likes/dislikes, and feelings, about 7% of the message is carried by words. Tone of voice accounts for 38%, and body language

accounts for the remaining 55% percent. Mehrabian, A. (1981). *Silent messages: Implicit communication of emotions and attitudes* (2nd ed.). Belmont, California: Wadsworth

6   Micro Expressions: Paul Ekman has made an extensive study of basic emotions across cultures. Each core emotion has specific muscles that are present in every culture. Ekman, P (2003) *Emotions Revealed*, New York: Times Books

7   Damasio, A (1999). *The Feeling of What Happens: Body and Emotion in the Making of Consciousness.* New York: Harcourt Brace

8   Boyatzis, R and McKee, A (2005). *Resonant Leadership: Renewing Yourself and Connecting with Others Through Mindfulness, Hope, and Compassion.* Boston: Harvard Business Press

9   Seligman, M (1991). *Learned Optimism: How to Change Your Mind and Your Life.* New York: Knopf. Note we use "Powerless" versus "Effort Possible." Seligman's third P is "Personal," but I find "Powerless" to be more clear.

10   Optimism and Health: In *Learned Optimism* Martin Seligman reports several studies on the link between health and optimism. We've corroborated these findings with the *Six Seconds Emotional Intelligence Assessment.* Freedman, Ghini, Fiedeldey-Van Dijk (2005), *Emotional Intelligence and Success*

11   Boyatzis, R and McKee, A (2005). *Resonant Leadership: Renewing Yourself and Connecting with Others Through Mindfulness, Hope, and Compassion.* Boston: Harvard Business Press

12   Seligman, M (1991). *Learned Optimism: How to Change Your Mind and Your Life.* New York: Knopf

Chapter Seven

Give Yourself:
From Success to Significance

George McCown is the Chairman of a private equity and management firm, McCown De Leeuw & Co. At their height, the company had $1.8 billion under management; since 1984, MDC has acquired and run 40 organizations, creating companies that today collectively generate in excess of $6 billion in annual sales.

How did they get there? McCown and his partners made a bold decision to create a unique mission: To build partnerships that make a difference. McCown says that at first they were really afraid — how could they go into hard-bitten Wall Street capitalists with that kind of "soft" mission? Then something surprising happened.

"We'd walk in and start talking about the mission," McCown recalls, "and these guys would get up and close the door and start talking about how that's what they've always wanted to be part of." When you connect your

*What would you do
if you were not afraid?*

- George McCown

daily actions with your deeper purpose, you become more compelling and engaging as a leader. You capture hearts and minds.

"Connecting with purpose" may sound lofty and idealistic – and even impractical in a day-to-day business sense. Today's popular culture is so focused on "me first" that the value of altruistic service is considered "fluffy." People have been conditioned to dismiss the whole concept of service to a larger ideal.

Yet nearly every person I've met has a deep yearning to contribute to the world. I guess there may be some out there who really don't care, but I've not found them. From hard bitten executives to Marines just back from Iraq to teens struggling to make it, from high powered salespeople at Schlumberger to moms in Jakarta, I hear this refrain over and over. Maybe they don't admit it at first, maybe they start by talking about material needs and getting good toys – but when I start asking them these bigger questions, the underlying motivation begins to show.

I remember talking to one businesswoman who insisted her whole purpose was making money. But when she started talking about the product her company sold, she spoke of bringing beauty and magic back into the world. Her eyes lit up and he became passionate and articulate about her work and its purpose.

I've seen this same dynamic with a huge range of people; from sheiks to street people, soldiers to scientists, money-driven salespeople to IT scientists, literally every single person I've spoken with has expressed that part of her/his motivation is to make a difference.

What difference do you want to make?

It's not an easy question. Maybe you've already thought about it, maybe this is a new idea, but take a moment now to consider it seriously. What are you adding to the world? In 100 years when your great-great-grandchildren talk about you, what will they say you passed onto them? What is your emotional legacy?

Why does it matter?

Maybe leadership has always been incredibly complex, but it seems even more so today. My clients around the world tell me that it's phenomenally difficult to succeed today. Between geopolitics and terror, global climate changes, increasing fuel costs, rapidly accelerating technology, and a brutally fast pace, organizations are struggling. Leaders are struggling. You are probably in a position where you are asking people to do more with less. And why should they?

I was working with a CEO of a healthcare company. His staff was deeply motivated by their sense of purpose, but for him the priority was fiscal. He who kept insisting, "People better dig deeper because if they don't, the company will close." Over and over I told him that his employees did not really care about the company's financial health — they cared about the customers whose lives they were saving.

"They better care," he'd say, "because they won't be able to do the work if we close the doors." The CEO was caught in a paradigm of scarcity and fear, and he thought he could motivate people that way. It may work for a short time, but then good people stop investing and they go work for the competition. The staff commitment to mission could have been a powerful lever for change, but he couldn't access that because he did not connect his work with the larger purpose. The company went into bankruptcy a year later.

Contrast that with Grant Bannen, the General Manager of the Sheraton Studio City in Orlando (see Chapter 3 for the case). Grant was brought in to turn the 500-bed hotel around. By nature a gruff and relentless perfectionist, it would have been easy for him to fall into the role of critic and task-master. He pushes himself just as hard as his staff; he's a hands-on leader and no task is beneath him – one day when a big group was arriving he took three managers and they spent the morning changing beds, this while he was suffering from severe arthritis.

Grant's success shows that emotionally intelligent leadership is about authenticity and commitment – not being "nice." As I described earlier in the book, I worked with Grant and his team for almost a year providing EQ consulting and training. Over the course of the year they increased market share by 24% and earned the highest guest-satisfaction scores in the history of the hotel. They won the Sheraton #1 rating for guest satisfaction in the vacation group in two of the three last months of the year. At the end of this incredible year, Grant stands up in front of the full staff and congratulates them, then goes back to the gruff: "But don't let it go to your heads. We have a lot of work to do here! The watchword for this year is 'no complacency.'"

Where a lot of leaders would alienate staff with a brusque and relentless style, Grant's people know he's demanding for a reason that's more powerful than financial success. Grant is driven by a genuine sense of caring. He wants guests to feel taken care of – it's a soul-deep commitment and you can see it even in the way he walks the halls. The staff has an incredible respect for "Mr. Grant," as they affectionately call him, because they know he is pushing for something that matters. Over and over each day, in hundreds of small one-to-one interactions, he shows staff how to take better care of guests. How to fulfill their purpose as hoteliers.

His commitment is contagious because he lives it every day, and the effect is powerful. As Grant wrote to me a few months ago, "While there are the inevitable fits and starts inherent in our volatile business, the trend continues up. We've now had more than 24 straight months of plus 100% market share; by the end of 2005 vs. 2003 (my first full year) total revenues will be up a minimum of 64% and gross operating profit up 429%; We'll be up 2005 vs. 2004 by 14.5% in revenues and 30.0% in profit (although hurricanes, fuel prices, etc. dampened the last two quarters of 2005)." In 2004 Grant was named GM of the Year and Sales and Catering teams were Kessler Teams of the Year.

Working for pay is not compelling enough today. If you want that extra discretionary effort, that commitment that will move your company toward world-class, then you need to offer your people a deeper motivation.

Resonant Leadership

In *Primal Leadership* Daniel Goleman, Richard Boyatzis and Annie McKee talk about resonant leadership, a concept Boyatzis and McKee carried forward as the title of their latest book. They describe leaders who develop a strong level of emotional influence by caring and committing. In their description, resonant leaders call on a group to dig deeper and go further simply because of an emotional connection. That's what the Give Yourself part of the model delivers.

Have you ever been in the room with a leader who really called that forth in you? Someone whose very presence invited you to be and do more – to take it higher? I was at a conference with several Nobel Peace Prize winners – Desmond Tutu (Archbishop who led South Africa's Peace and Reconciliation process), Oscar Arias (President who unilaterally disarmed Costa Rica), and Jody Williams (led the International Campaign to Ban Landmines) – and I viscerally experienced the pull of purpose. Someone who is truly "living on purpose" has a significant gravitational pull. When s/he stands in front of a group, people just want to be part of it. That's an incredibly powerful kind of influence.

I'm not talking about the "cult of personality" kind of leader that was popular in the 90s. This form of leadership does not come because of glamour or the trappings of status. As Robert Cooper asks, "If you did not have the title and the corner office, would anyone still follow you?" Why would they? Why have they? I suspect a large part of it is that you connect with your own passion and purpose in a way that gives them hope to do the same.

I've seen this kind of leadership with a few members of the US military. The Chief of Chaplains for the US Navy, Admiral Robert Burt, is this kind of leader. He walks into a room and eyes just go toward him – eyes and hearts. He stands in front of a group and talks for a few minutes, no notes, no charts – just him, fully present, alive, and in service to an imperative mission (bringing spiritual presence and wisdom to the warriors who risk their lives for our nation). Again, it's a soul-deep commitment, and while he is an articulate speaker and a smart man, it's not the words that matter: It's the spirit, the heart beneath those words.

It's what I strive for as a leader. I am not a leader because of a title or position, whatever leadership I have is given to me by others – because I influence them. I help run an international organization with hundreds of people spread all over the world. I don't sign these people's checks, I don't have positional power. All I have is influence – influence they gift to me because they see something in me, they see me serving a commitment that we share.

One of the best compliments I ever got was from a guy named Norm. We were working together on one of those projects that can just suck the life out of you – an infinite amount of work dawn to dusk. I was an outside consultant and Norm was a senior manager. We spent quite a few hours together getting the right processes working in the right ways – aligning mission, systems, and people. A great deal of my time was influencing people to lead in an emotionally intelligent way. Through dialogue, strategic planning, and training exercises, I asked people to Know Themselves and be real about what they were feeling and what was happening. Then we worked to help them see the options so they could Choose Themselves. Finally we kept coming back to the organization's compelling purpose for existence, and over and over I asked people to connect their choices with that mission – to Give Themselves.

In this kind of long-term change process, it can be hard to see if your efforts are working. You have to keep a lot of different balls in the air at the same time, and it can feel chaotic. Late one night we were driving back to the hotel, talking about this challenge, and Norm said out of the blue, "Josh, you are a good man and a good leader and I would walk into a burning building for you." It wasn't so much the words, of course, it was the emotional impact. We had connected around purpose – each of us doing work that matters deeply, and calling on others to do the same. And because Norm was in touch with his emotions (Know Yourself), he decided to use that emotion rather than hide it (Choose Yourself), plus he did so with empathy and purpose (Give Yourself). So I know from my own experience

*Until he extends his
circle of compassion
to include all living things,
man will not himself find peace.*

— Albert Schweitzer
(1875 - 1965)

that when people interact in this way it changes them – it's changed me. Sometimes, years later, when I'm struggling to be true to my core, I ask myself about Norm's burning building. I strive to be worthy of that kind of trust, and I do so by measuring my decisions against my own Noble Goal. When I lead in this way, I enroll people to go further.

Let me be clear though – much of the time, maybe even most of the time, that takes effort. And I don't succeed all the time. I take comfort from baseball: a world-record batter hits four out of 10 balls. If I'm batting over 300 that's enough for the major leagues. The goal isn't perfection: It's growth.

Elusive Empathy

Empathy is both one of the most powerful EQ leadership competencies, and one of the most challenging. Empathy means making space for someone's feelings and connecting with them on an emotional level so they feel understood, safe, and respected.

Empathy feels like acceptance, trust, listening, and caring all at once. It's nonjudgmental, patient, and serious. Have you felt empathy from someone else? Can you remember how that affected you? How it increased your trust with and commitment to the other person?

There is a beautiful paradox to empathy that makes it illusive. When you try to make someone feel cared about

EQ Competency:
Increase Empathy

Empathy is the ability to recognize and appropriately respond to other people's emotions. It is a nonjudgmental openness to others' feelings and experiences that builds connection and awareness.

As a leader, Increasing Empathy is key to understanding others and forming enduring and trusting relationships. Leaders who are not empathic may miss critical insight into others and can be seen as self-interested, cold, or not trustworthy.

because you want something, or because you "should," or because if you hurry up and listen for a minute they'll be quiet and listen to you, it just does not work. Empathy is subtle and fragile. It's destroyed by insincerity and egotism.

On the other hand, it is incredibly easy! You were born empathic – at just a few months of age babies will provide a comforting touch to someone who is sad. It's the most natural, effortless response to another person's struggle or joy. We just have to get out of our own way.

Personally, I've had to work hard on empathy. I'm impatient and results oriented, and strong emotions frighten me. So it has taken a lot of practice to just sit still and feel. My own experience is that to be more empathic I just need to close my mouth and open my ears and my heart. Again, empathy is part of "Give Yourself" because it only really works when you are, at some level, sacrificing for another person. It takes committed vulnerability to really connect in this way.

Empathy can grow from just recognizing the challenge or pain someone is facing. It's a guide that can help us relate to others, and it has the bottom-line value of building collaboration. It also helps by keeping our decisions serving the greater good; in some ways, empathy is the antidote to egotism.

I wish that I was more adept at empathy in my own daily work and life. I find that it often feels better (for a moment) to be annoyed with people than to empathize with them.

For example, recently I was having trouble negotiating an agreement. Quickly I started to feel frustrated, defensive, and angry. I thought I was being taken advantage of, and I began to blame the other parties.

My pattern when I think an "opponent" is not listening is to seek to diminish him, minimize his importance, and rally allies to my just and righteous point of view. Ok, it hurts to write that – but not as bad as this: I like the feelings that come with that "attacking back."

Of course I do! After all, I'm telling myself that I'm being taken advantage of, that they don't appreciate me and my team, that they're not listening. I am afraid they will hurt me, so I want to hurt them harder, faster, and deeper. This impulse comes from a visceral drive to avoid being a victim. So, I let that fear drive my ego into action, and I get up on my high horse. From there, I get to pretend that I am powerful, wise, and indispensable.

Ironically, that very behavior turns me into a victim of my own patterns because it pushes me to solidify the belief that they are trying to take advantage of me. To strengthen my feeling of being right, I also have to strengthen my belief that I am under attack.

A curious cycle occurs in these moments. A friend called it "jerk-inertia." You start acting like a jerk, and it kind of feels good, so you keep doing it.

This biggest challenge is the way the inertia builds on itself. The more I act protecting my ego, proving myself right over others, the more I get to be righteous – and the more I enjoy the certainty that comes from being a victim and "knowing" I am right. Soon, there is a double loss if I were to stop the behavior. First, I lose the seductive illusion of power and "rightness." Second, I might have to feel really bad about what a jerk I've been, so I have even more drive to keep going.

At the same time, some other part of myself is screaming in anguish knowing that my jerk-persona is making incredibly stupid mistakes that move me away from my true goals. Each jerk-sustaining action (those that increase the jerk-inertia) moves me further into a morass, moves me further from truly understanding the people with whom I disagree, and moves both of us further into position as circling boxers looking for an opening to exploit.

I find that my curiosity helps me shift off the slippery slope. I start wondering what's really going on for the other people. Then I begin to empathize as I attempt to understand. When I get curious, I start to look for clues; I review their words, I consider their body language, and I begin to gain new perspective.

In my work as a facilitator I have the privilege of working with all kinds of groups to improve communication. My job is to help them find ways of understanding, and I have only two tools that make a difference. The first is the ability to ask questions. The second is empathy.

After these sessions, people often ask me how I am able to facilitate challenging discussions and make it safe for people. I'm not totally sure, but while I am often impatient inside, and while I prefer to leap to solutions and actions, beneath it I deeply care about their feelings. Maybe it's just good imagination: I often see myself in their positions, and I feel an approximation of what that's like; in other words, I empathize. When I let that empathy drive me I am far more effective.

Perhaps the most useful advice is to be clear about your goals. If you want to resolve issues in ways that form long-term partnerships, then you'll always look to see the situation through the other person's eyes. Empathy is the key to finding lasting solutions.

Five Steps to Empathy

Anabel Jensen, Ph.D., is the President of Six Seconds and someone who is incredibly good at empathy. Anabel identifies five steps to empathy:

1. Recognize Body Language: There are signs, or signals, that tell us about other people's feelings. Just as in emotional literacy, these signals give us insight into others' emotional worlds.

2. Listen: Most corporate training on listening focuses on "listening to ideas." Take it a step further and listen to the person's heart. What is s/he saying that's not even in the words? To listen you must be quiet – it is why we have two ears and one mouth.

3. Notice the Pain: Beneath the words and the posture, a person needs empathy because of some emotional hurt. You may never have felt that hurt exactly, but

maybe you have felt something similar. Maybe they are feeling the hurt of a child dying and you don't have children – but can you remember when a friend or family member died?

4. Respond Verbally: Use your words to mirror back what they are saying; validate their experience (even if you disagree or it does not make sense to you yet – it is still real for them). Don't say, "I know what you are experiencing" – you don't.

5. Respond with Action: The words alone do not "close the deal" on empathy. If you are truly empathizing, you must act. Sometimes the action is as simple as sitting still longer, looking at the person, smiling gently. Sometimes it is more visible, but the empathic action is not about problem solving, it is about emotional connection. Be careful not to "fix" a problem that is not yours.

Deep Acting

Pursuing a Noble Goal is clearly an important part of leadership, but what does it have to do with emotional intelligence?

Emotions researchers talk about two kinds of emotion management. "Surface acting" is an effort of will where you force yourself to suppress an impulse. You want to scream at someone but you stifle that and say something banal and "polite."

Surface acting is a social necessity, and in many places, such as Asia, a cultural imperative. But it comes at a price. First, surface acting requires a kind of effort called "emotional labor." It is stress-inducing. When you do a lot of surface acting you become exhausted and you don't have energy available for leading.

Second, everyone knows you're faking it. People think of themselves as masterful liars, but few actually are. In Paul Ekman's work on emotional expression, he's shown that there are hundreds of tiny expressions crossing a person's face every few minutes. These microexpressions reveal the underlying emotional message loud and clear to anyone paying attention.

In our trainings we sometimes video tape a frustrating interaction and then ask the participants to talk about their feelings. Due to social convention, they typically minimize the intensity of their feelings, saying something like, "Well, I guess I was a little bit annoyed, but just for a second." Then we play back the scene in slow motion. The face clearly shows intense annoyance.

So, when you control your emotions through surface acting you exhaust yourself and you lose credibility. People may respect your restraint, but they will know your reaction for what it is.

The alternative is deep acting. In deep acting, you actually transform the feelings. You shift from frustration to appreciation, from impatience to empathy, from judgment to curiosity. It can happen in a matter of seconds, and it can be efficient and worth the energy expended. The advantage of deep acting is that it actually gives you energy and makes you more authentic. But how do you do it?

A Noble Goal is a highly effective tool. Let me go back to George McCown. George is brilliant intellectually and he can be really impatient. So when someone irritates him, it's easy for George to verbally tear that person apart. He learned to suppress the response with surface acting, but he was not getting the kind of results he really wanted.

When he developed a Noble Goal, he found a lever that would move him out of this pattern. George's Noble Goal is "To make others good." That means his enduring commitment is to support himself and others to be the best they can, and functionally it means being less judgmental by seeing the good in everyone. When George does that, he can instantly shift from impatience and judgment to curiosity and empathy. You can see him do it – it's like a light switches on inside and his whole attitude changes.

Nelson Mandela is an incredible example of this. Here is a man who spent most of his life persecuted and imprisoned, yet he did not get stuck in feelings of anger and fear. Of course he must have experienced those feelings at times in his life, but because he had a deep purpose of co-creating a free and just nation, he was able to transform the feelings into a magnetic personal power; a power based on influence and relationship.

EQ Competency:
Pursue Noble Goals

Noble goals activate all of the other elements of EQ. By connecting with our sense of purpose, the commitment to emotional intelligence gains relevance and power. Just as our personal priorities shape our daily choices, our Noble Goals shape our long-term choices. They give us a sense of direction, a 'north star' to calibrate our compass, and they help us align our thinking, feeling, and acting to maintain integrity.

As a leader, Pursuing a Noble Goal helps you fully engage commitment, lets you truly transform your emotions at a deep level, influence others most effectively, and maintain your own energy and drive. Leaders who do not have this skill may burn out or have trouble persevering through challenge. Others may not commit to them, and they probably won't inspire peak performance from their teams. High scores on Noble Goals also predict quality of relationships — and business people with high scores here are almost twice as likely to be senior leaders.

So a Noble Goal is a tool for emotional self-mastery. It frees you from the prison of reactivity, it motivates you to be and do your best, and it strengthens your personal power to engage, influence, and inspire others.

In the film *Celebrate What's Right With the World*, Dewitt Jones talks about making a shift from success to significance. What is the significance you choose to have? How can you put that into action today and every day?

When we Know Ourselves and become more emotionally self-aware, then we Choose Ourselves and move to a calm step of the escalator, and Give Ourselves and connect with purpose, we've established a virtuous, self-reinforcing spiral. The more we Know, Choose, and Give ourselves, the better able we are to strengthen and deepen in the other areas.

Emotions become profoundly important guides, signals, that help us live our values every day. As a result, we become more focused, more persuasive, more inspiring, and we feel better and better ourselves. As we cycle through this EQ tool, spinning the propeller, we gain focus, strength, and integrity to truly lead.

Constructing a Noble Goal

A Noble Goal is a brief and compelling statement of purpose that helps you evaluate your choices. Beyond a "mission statement," a Noble Goal encompasses all aspects of your life (personal, work, community, etc.) and inspires you to

It is not enough to be busy;
so are the ants.

The question is:
What are we busy about?

— Henry David Thoreau

live your best. To be a Noble Goal, your statement will meet these criteria:

- Integrating - it encompasses all dimensions of your life; serving your Noble Goal in one domain (such as work) supports you in all others (such as family). This helps you find balance.

- Gets you out of bed - it motivates and inspires you at a deep level; this helps you find the energy when the going gets tough.

- Pointed outward - while you will benefit, the focus is on others. This helps you maintain an expansive vision.

- Not complete in your lifetime - it is enduring and inspiring, something beyond the daily struggle. This helps you maintain a long-term focus so you can avoid the confusion of short-term thinking.

- Ennobles vs. diminishes others – no one has to be "less than" or "wrong" for you to pursue your Noble Goal; this helps you stay out of ego and power struggle.

I first learned about the significance of a Noble Goal from Claire Nuer, a holocaust and cancer survivor who became a transformational teacher and creator of an organization called Learning as Leadership. Claire's Noble Goal was, "To co-create a context for humanity," a context where people could fully develop as compassionate, wise creatures. We adapted the concept from Claire and her team and are deeply grateful for their teaching.

Karen McCown, the founding Chairman of Six Seconds, has a Noble Goal that's been the cornerstone of all our work. Her Noble Goal is to "Support myself and others to be human beings," (as opposed to humans having). This focuses Karen on what truly nourishes and sustains the highest good. She uses this as a yardstick for her decisions, in turn influencing the organization to nurture the essential dignity and goodness of all people. Now many thousands of people have been "infected by this virus" of this commitment.

Values in Action

Your Noble Goal needs to align with your values and principles. It should give you force, a driving engine, to put your core values into action (versus leaving them on a fancy plaque or card in your wallet).

What are your values? What's important to you? One way of reflecting on values and principles is to consider an ethical dilemma.

For example, consider this situation:

> Albert has taken over sales operations for a financial services company with very tight margins. One of the most important referral sources is a group of professional accountants.

These accountants have come to expect first-class treatment from the company – expensive meals, preferential business treatment, and even inside information. While the relationship does not usually break any laws, Albert questions the COO because these accountants seem to have undue influence.

How should the COO respond?

Now, reflect on your answer to identify what values it conveys. If you said, "COO should tell Albert to treat them like all others," then you probably value equity or fairness. If you said, "Maintain harmony in the relationship," perhaps you value relationships or saving face. Which of these values do you see prominent in your answer?

relationship	harmony/face	profitability
equity	balance	security
human spirit	winning	strength
humility	openness	protectiveness
partnership	hope	pride

You can also consider what principles you would apply. A principle is a rule or law that lets you apply the values. If you value relationship, the principle might be, "To maintain harmonious relations." If you value winning, the principle might be, "To seek the most gain."

Integrating the Domains

To reflect on the "integrate all domains" aspect of your noble goal, imagine you have a year sabbatical coming up. Your basic expenses are covered for the year. What will you do with the time?

You have 50 weeks to allocate – where will you put your time? Fill in this chart with important activities:

Don't read further - take a moment and write down your answer in the chart on the next page. Write what you really think, there is no wrong answer!

Area	How many weeks:	Important objectives/ activities:
Career		
Family		
Spirit / Health		
Friends / Community		
Other		

Now, look at the chart above, and consider what themes you see. Are there topics that you see in multiple columns?

List the 3-4 important themes:

Next, go back to one of the items on the chart that seems important to you. Answer these three questions, adapted from creativity guru Michael Ray:

1. Why is that important? *(write it down)*

2. And what difference would that (your #1 answer) make? *(write it down)*

3. And how would that (answer to #2) help you meet your purpose?

Repeat for 3-4 different items from the chart.

Next, imagine your retirement party. You are leaving the company and you overhear a group of direct-reports talking in the hall. They are talking about the way you've affected them. What do you hope they are saying? *(write it down)*

Finally, to make it more personal, take a few days to work on the answer to this question:

> When my great grandchildren talk
> about me, what do I want them to say?

Putting it Together

Now, reflect on your values and principles, the themes for your "sabbatical" year, the reasons that is important, and the legacy you want to leave, and begin to craft a short, compelling statement.

You may wish to use one of these verbs or one like this:

inspire	support	engage
enrich	nurture	nourish
learn	practice	model
enhance	co-create	foster
enroll	be	preserve

Write a draft of your Noble Goal:

Finally, return to the five criteria listed above and check that your statement meets all the criteria. Continue to revise to a brief, compelling statement. This can take some time, but the results are worth it!

Leading with Your Noble Goal

Once you have developed a clear statement of your Noble Goal, it will be invaluable in your leadership. Your Noble Goal will help you manage your reactions so you can be and do your best, gain the energy you need to manage change, and it will clarify your decision making process.

Reactions: When you find yourself falling into unconscious patterns, check that against your Noble Goal. "Is this pattern serving my ego, or my Noble Goal?" It's a simple way to assess your own behavior. Do it every evening – look back over the day and review your actions. In what parts of your day were you truly at your best? When were you serving your Noble Goal and when were you undermining it? Each day is a new chance to practice.

Energy: It takes a tremendous amount of energy to lead. To keep connecting with people, moving fast, responding to the hundreds of requests that cross your desk, you need a burning fire within you. Exercise, a good diet, and optimism also help fuel that, but none of those suffice without a Noble Goal. Put in action to increase excitement, hope, and commitment: As you look at the work you do each day, find small and large ways to link those to your Noble Goal. For example, if your Noble Goal is to "To inspire respect and peace," and you have to do performance reviews, consider how to do those in a way that's adding respect and peace to the world. Every day you add something to the world – if you do that in alignment with your Noble Goal, you'll find more and more energy to live and lead.

Decision making. You make dozens, even hundreds, or choices each day – some small, some monumental. Often it's challenging to see which option really makes most sense, there is logic on both sides, and emotion as well. So how do you choose the direction? Which is most in line with your Noble Goal? Which is most in line with the Noble Goal of the organization or the other people in the situation? If you don't see, or have not been presented with, an option that serves your Noble Goal, insist on identifying more options. You will find that when you make decisions from this deepest set of principles, profit and success follow automatically. Sometimes it takes longer, but the results are also more enduring.

Chapter Seven Recap

Key Concept:

Giving of yourself, both through your Noble Goal and by empathizing, increases your self-mastery, your influence, and your wisdom.

Related Reading:

True North: Discover Your Authentic Leadership, Bill George and Peter Sims

Reclaiming Higher Ground: Creating Organizations that Inspire the Soul, Lance Secretan

The 8th Habit, Stephen Covey

Key Practice:

Connect with your Noble Goal. Reminding yourself of your Noble Goal on a regular basis will increase your commitment to be and do your best. You can use it as a yardstick for all decisions: "What will support my Noble Goal – and other's?"

Chapter Eight

Organizational Excellence: The Climate for Performance[1]

So far we've been looking primarily at emotional intelligence and how it relates to you as an individual leader. The majority of this book has focused on illustrating the Six Seconds EQ Model and how these competencies affect you and your leadership. Understanding EQ on the personal level is an important first step, and there are two more levels as we move to look at EQ for teams and for organizations.

To become expert at leading with emotional intelligence, it's necessary to see and manage emotions on three levels:

- Individual (ourselves),

- Relational (those we encounter on a regular basis), and

- Organizational (the larger system).

Each affects the others. Every decision, every incident, every interaction at one level has implications on the

Figure 8.1: Three Levels

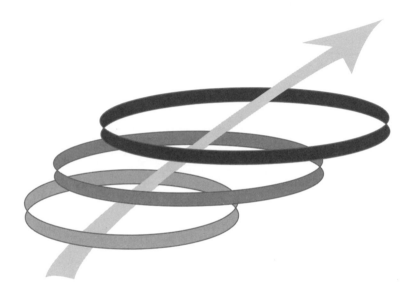

To master emotionally intelligent leadership it is necessary to become skilled at monitoring and managing emotions on all three levels: Individual (smallest), Relational (medium), and Organizational (largest).

What are your feelings? The team's? The organizational climate? What are the implications of a decision or plan on all three levels?

Each affects the others. Are all three aligned?

others. An individual comes into work late. The people on her team are frustrated. These people interact with a hundred people across the organization – the one action ripples outward. It happens the other way too – a new strategic plan causes a team to change direction, one team member is hurt by the decision and loses productivity. As a leader, you are responsible for all three – and tuning into your own EQ will give you the tools to understand and manage the other two levels.

In the current business context discussed in chapter three, in the churn of today's business, most teams are facing more work with less people; the remaining people are frequently "running on empty" as they struggle to adapt. What leadership alchemy does it take to engage people to dig deeper and reach further quarter after quarter? Just as an individual's emotions affect his performance, the emotional tone, or climate, of the organization drives group behavior.

We can measure individual EQ and we can measure how individual competencies play out into the collective set of emotions and reactions that shape the organizational climate. By the way, when I use the term "climate," think of the weather report. The culture is a set of rules that tell people how they're supposed to behave. The climate is how they feel about it.

Our research on organization climate shows a powerful link between feelings and performance. Assessing customer service, productivity, and retention, our most recent study found that 57.7% of the difference between low and high performance is predicted by our climate factors.[2] In other words, climate is a bell-weather for financial and programmatic success.

The study examined responses from 395 people from entry level workers to CEOs and ages from 20s to 60s; they work in education, industry, government, and service businesses. Just over half the subjects were from the US, others from Europe, Canada, Asia, Latin America, and Africa. The demographics were thoroughly scrutinized to detect how they might impact organizational climate or job performance and we found only minor demographic skews; climate cuts across all these boundaries.

In addition to asking about the climate in their workplace, we asked about four important business factors:

- Customer Service – perception that customers are well cared for.

- Results – perception that work is done efficiently and the right work is done.

- Retention – keeping employees.

- Future Success – stainability of performance.

Organizational climate scores are extremely strong predictors of scores on these outcomes. In other words: **when employees feel good about coming to work, they perform better**. Conversely, when they are disengaged, frustrated, disappointed, or discontented, energy drops, quality suffers, communication is compromised, and good people start looking to leave the organization. These disengaged feelings are costly – both in immediate financial loss and in longer-term impact on the organization's reputation that come with reduced quality and lost customer/client relationships. Fortunately, there are sophisticated, low cost, and creative methods to improve and maintain this essential area of organizational viability.

To illustrate this challenge, let's look at two fictional employees on their way to work:

> Carl is looking forward to doing his best work; he's engaged and excited. Partly because he's "just a positive guy," and partly because he's part of a great team – his boss listens, the work seems to matter, and his team is supportive.

> Joan is dreading another day on the grindstone. She's experienced, skilled, and a good worker, but there are some things about this organization that rub her the wrong way. She doesn't think her boss cares, and she's just not connecting with the team.

How will they each perform today? How will they affect others? And what do they each need to remain productive and engaged?

A knee-jerk response might be to deliver a hard message to Joan and make it clear it's time to get with the program or get out. While this is a conventional response, it is

Figure 8.2: Performance Vital Signs

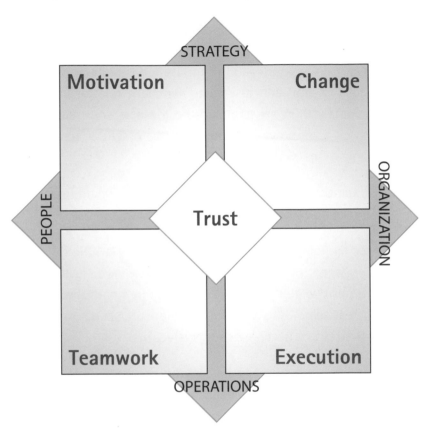

The Vital Signs Model, above, defines "High Performance" for individual leadership, teams, and organizations. The five climate factors in the middle predict the outcomes at the four "arrows":

Strategy: *We know where we're going.*

Organizations: *We have the systems to go there.*

Operations: *We are taking steps to move forward.*

People: *Our employees are coming too.*

unlikely to gain Joan's commitment. In *Change or Die*, Alan Deutschman makes the case that force, facts, and fear don't lead to change. Instead, change begins with a relationship.

Based on our research across hundreds of organizations and dozens of countries, there are specific drivers that will provide a tremendous improvement in Joan's performance, and different drivers that will keep Carl's high level of energy and commitment.[3]

The first requirement is for organizational leaders to commit that a healthy and positive climate is a strategic priority. Today, the "people side" is not a "soft" area that gets attention when business is booming. Climate is one of the top, if not the highest, priority of the best leaders. Great leaders provide a "container" that incubates exceptional performance.

"Why didn't I know??"

All too often, leaders become isolated from their teams – they don't have close relationships with the people two or three layers down. This gap can easily become a source of distrust and organizational dysfunction that impinges on the organization's ability to provide superior services. In dozens of administrations of our Organizational Vital Signs assessment, we've seen massive gaps between senior leaders', managers', and employees' perceptions. While not necessarily a problem in itself, this gap is a warning sign.

Employees frequently tell us they don't know their top leaders. Leaders tell us they feel disconnected from the front line. Unfortunately, this isolation is usually accompanied by a loss of trust and performance. All too often the people at the top of the organization receive "filtered" information – when more than anyone else, executives need the real story.

Leaders need to hear the "voice of the people," not a biased perception filtered through layers of management. And they need to hear it on a regular basis. Would a manufacturing company only check their quality metrics once a year? Would a sales organization only check their conversion rate biannually? No, because they run the organization on these metrics. Likewise, climate metrics should be part of the regular "dashboard" for evaluating the organization's health.

A validated, normed employee survey is an excellent way to gather unbiased opinion. The Organizational Vital Signs (OVS) climate assessment has been designed, tested and validated to help executives re-connect with their employees and identify opportunities to improve organizational climate. The assessment is called "Vital Signs" because it helps leaders keep their fingers on the pulse of the organization.

Understanding the climate lets leaders into the hearts and minds of their people. With this insight they can make more effective decisions about their own leadership as well as set strategic direction for improvement.

We've developed the "Vital Signs Model" (see Figure 8.2) to define the components of high performance – for leaders, teams, and organizational climate. The factors are:

- **Motivation** is the source of energy to overcome challenges, pursue a goal, or maintain commitment.

- **Change** is the readiness to innovate and adapt to succeed in a continuously evolving situation.

- **Teamwork** is collaborating to pursue a goal; it requires a sense of shared purpose and belonging.

- **Execution** is the ability to achieve strategic results by implementing effective tactics.

As shown in Figure 8.2, these are "bolted together" with a central, essential driver that unifies the model:

- **Trust** is a feeling of confidence, faith, and surety that engenders a willingness to risk and facilitates success in the other climate factors.

The Vital Signs Model provides a structure for understanding the key ingredients of leadership, and the responsibilities of the leader in creating a context for performance.

Now I Know!

How much does climate matter? Our research shows that trust alone predicts 46% of the difference between low and high performance. In the area of customer service, 37.9% is predicted by trust. Grouped together the climate factors predict around 50% in the variation of the four key organizational outcomes:

- Customer Service
- Results
- Retention
- Future Success

In other words: **Improving the organizational climate is likely to offer significant benefits** to your ability to meet your mission and achieve your financial success.

Sherry Thornton was the COO of one of the healthcare organizations we researched. She intuitively saw the gap between departments and between management and line, so we quantified the issues for her with the climate assessment. Everyone in the organization was invited to take the survey, and we conducted one-to-one structured interviews with a random sampling of around 10% of employees. Then we traveled to each site and had an "all hands" meeting with Thornton and other members of the leadership team. These meetings focused first on showing the team members that their input was going all the way to the top of the organization – that leadership was listening. "The Organizational Vital Signs process helped focus our change effort and increased buy-in from staff," says Thornton. Sharing the results with each facility team, staff "felt heard" and could support efforts to improve the workplace environment.

After measuring the climate and finding a need for improved accountability and collaboration, we focused leaders on connecting and following through in an "emotionally intelligent" way. Walking through a facility and eating lunch with line staff is not enough – both intention and action are required. Thornton executed a simple strategy: Listen to people, identify their needs, commit to meet the needs, and then deliver. At the same time as tactical needs are being met, attention to the underlying emotional needs is key. Employees who care about their jobs and their clients have good ideas, they are committed, they want to be part of the team, and they want you to hear them.

After 11 months of training, coaching, and effort by the executive team, census (sales) increased by over 25%, while incidents, accidents and operating costs where significantly reduced. Six Seconds helped the management team develop and use emotional intelligence to better understand their organization and connect more effectively with their people – thereby improving the bottom line.

One Size Fits All?

While a generally positive climate helps, our research shows that targeted efforts are the most productive – different groups have very different drivers for performance.

In one study, we examined how climate influences customer service. To understand how climate affects groups differently, we compared satisfied versus dissatisfied employees.

We found that different groups in the study have very different predictors for performance. For example, for the group that is least satisfied with the organizational climate overall, collaboration predicts almost 30% of customer service. By contrast, collaboration only accounts for 3% among people who are satisfied – for this group alignment (having a connection with the organization's mission) is by far the most important factor. This kind of sophisticated analysis allows us to tailor training and development so learning solves an organizational problem (rather than being a "box to check" that training is being done).

For example, let's go back to "Joan" and "Carl" and see what will improve their customer service. If they worked in the organization we analyzed above:

- For dissatisfied employees like Joan, **collaboration** is the key to customer service – it predicts 30% of this group's customer service score.

- But for engaged people like Carl, collaboration only accounts for 3%. For this group **alignment** (having a connection with the organization's mission) is by far the most important factor.

In other words, understanding the climate of different groups lets a leader make tactical decisions focused on the real drivers of performance. Rather than a one size fits all approach, an in-depth understanding of climate lets leaders customize their interventions to get better results with less wasted time and effort.

Implementation Strategies

The focus of Six Seconds' consulting and training is to partner with leaders to develop thriving organizations. We don't believe there is a "cookie cutter" approach to getting great results, but seeing how other organizations have approached EQ may be useful in generating ideas. Here are five strategies we've applied with five organizations:

1. Direct Training – Oilfield Services

2. Train the Trainer - HSBC

3. Combined Training – US Navy

4. Integrated Tools – FedEx

5. Consulting Process – CIBA Chemical

For more on these and other examples, see the case library at www.6seconds.org/tag/case-study

Direct Training: The approach we're using with one of the world's largest Oilfield Services companies requires the least investment; it's where many organizations start. The company has an intensive Sales University for new account managers. In one division, an executive recognized the importance of the "human side" of sales and engaged us to deliver The Heart of Selling, a 2-day program designed for strategic, customer-oriented salespeople to focus on "how they are" with clients. We've now delivered the program to four Sales University classes to rave reviews (9.57/10).

Advantages: low risk, rapid deployment, and low upfront cost.

Disadvantages: lack of comprehensive follow-through / not integrated with overall human capital strategy.

Train the Trainer: To increase effectiveness in a diverse, complex global organization, the HSBC learning organization in Asia undertook to integrate EQ into their leadership development. Several members of the Learning & Development Department joined the Six Seconds' Network by attending our EQ Certification and our SEI EQ Assessment Certification. Then, in collaboration with Dr. Granville D'Souza in our Singapore office, they developed a pilot program. D'Souza delivered the pilot, they refined the program, then he conducted a series of Train-the-Trainer programs (with periodic review and coaching sessions to maintain quality). Now the HSBC trainers are delivering the customized, proven program and adding this "strand of EQ DNA" to the leadership culture.

Advantages: effective integration into the leadership development strategy. A larger group of certified facilitators builds organizational capacity (these tools can be used in a variety of trainings) which helps make it sustainable. Using the assessment tools helps measure return on investment and maintain focus.

Disadvantages: higher cost of entry and the need for / dependence on internal expertise.

Combined Training: To assist the United States Navy, Marine Corps, and Coast Guard meet a strategic priority of becoming more effective at change, the Chaplain Corps undertook a two-year initiative. The program began with a 2-day "Inside Path to Change" training for a group of senior officers involved in learning/organizational development. Similar to the HSBC case, Six Seconds was then contracted to customize the program into a 1-day introduction suited to the organization's unique needs. A Train-the-Trainer equipped a team of 24 internal trainers to deliver the one day program. The Train-the-Trainer was professionally video-taped to provide materials for a licensed distance-learning program to supplement the in-person program. The final phase of the project was a collaboration between the Navy's internal trainers (who we'd trained) and Six Seconds' experts to deliver a 40-hour blended program (elearning plus in-person) for 1000 officers and support personnel. The program included an array of tools licensed for use throughout the Sea Services so Chaplains can customize and bring these concepts to many of the 500,000 members of their organization.

Advantages: phased implementation after proof-of-concept. Development of organizational capacity; lets internal experts adapt materials for use in their unique context. The expanded use of external experts provides a more direct experience for a larger group of leaders increasing the likelihood that concepts can be integrated.

Disadvantages: a lack of comprehensive metrics (which could not be included due to financial constraints) and the significant investment in time and resources to roll-out a program of this scope.

Integrated Tools: One of the core values at FedEx is "people-first leadership." At the same time, it's an extremely fast-paced, operative company. At FedEx Express, the Global Learning Institute decided to incorporate emotional intelligence into their core learning programs. Over several years, numerous internal learning experts have attended many of Six Seconds' certifications and we've conducted programs in-house.

Primarily driven by their internal program designers, they've integrated EQ and various Six Seconds' assessment and development tools into two of the core programs, including a six-month development process for every new Express manager worldwide – a powerful example of "people-first leadership" in itself. This flagship program includes pre-assessment, training, coaching, and then re-assessment to track growth. Two of their most experienced facilitators have earned Six Seconds' Master Trainer status and are delivering Train-the-Trainer programs internally; now there are over 30 of their L&D professionals around the world certified in the SEI Assessment.

This strategy was staged over several years, starting with a small investment in a pilot, then growing after proof-of-concept.

Advantages: low-cost entry, solid metrics to identify the efficacy of their development approach, and a totally customizable process.

Disadvantages: relies on internal expertise (very high in this case).

Consulting Process: CIBA Specialty Chemicals is a leading global chemical company. Like many organizations they are continually looking for competitive advantage. At their largest plant in Italy, the Site Manager Luigi Boaretto has begun looking to implement emotional intelligence strategies to improve effectiveness while executing major changes including introducing SAP and implementing Lean Manufacturing Transformation.

Using a coach and consultant from Six Seconds, he is assessing "touch points" where emotional communication occurs inside the organization and between the organization and the stakeholders The focus is on considering and managing the emotional aspects alongside the rational ones. Emotional intelligence is helping produce excellent results by reducing resistance to change, minimizing talent retention issues, and amplifying results in the "value extraction" phase. Training and coaching for key managers are helping to increase awareness and reinforce the importance of managing the emotional elements, while outdoor activities, an organizational climate survey, and mentoring by key managers are building skills and awareness for the middle management population.

Advantages: long-term benefit; fully integrates into the organization; and makes emotional intelligence a "natural" part of the organization's culture.

Disadvantages: requires ongoing commitment.

Putting it Together: EQ in Action

So far we've seen that emotional intelligence skills enable leaders to work more effectively with people – which lets them create a great organizational climate. Climate has a major effect on performance. A tool like OVS (the Organizational Vital Signs assessment) helps measure the climate and provides a benchmark – but how do you improve it?

First, it helps to recognize that organizational climate arises from a web of individual relationships and feelings. Traditional leadership and management skills (such as charisma, decisiveness, financial acuity, tactical planning) are less significant and effective in dealing with climate factors. Instead, emotional intelligence skills are key because high EQ leaders "look beneath the surface" at the emotional drivers. What we can measure with the OVS, high EQ leaders perceive in real-time.

Let's go back to Carl and Joan. What are they feeling? What feelings will let them excel? In some organizations, the knee-jerk response is "fire Joan, hire someone like Carl!" Sometimes that is the best answer, but more often it's not. If we accept that emotions provide useful data, Joan's frustration is an asset. It's certainly data, and it might even be a force that can be harnessed to make positive change.

In many organizations, her dissatisfaction would lead people to isolate her – the exact opposite of the emotionally intelligent response. As we learned from the OVS analysis, collaboration is a driver for people like Joan. She probably doesn't feel connected to her team. It might be a bad fit, or it might be that Joan's feelings are a signal that something is not working well in the team. Between your survey results and your own emotional awareness, you'll begin to see what's really happening with Joan and you can then address the root cause of this issue. Suppose you are the manager; you can use the KCG model to design an effective response:

Know Yourself: You feel impatient with Joan and distrust her. You recognize a pattern in the team, which is when people are dissatisfied they are isolated.

Choose Yourself: Is Joan's concern really a personal attack on you? Maybe not. Doing the Consequential Thinking, you see that if you just fire Joan without dealing with the underlying issue then the "new Joan" has a similar problem. It seems like a pain to go through the process, but with Optimism it's possible.

Give Yourself: What's the experience like for Joan? She's isolated, not because she's bad, but because she wants something better for herself and for the team. Considering your own Noble Goal and the organization's, it is clear that you need to engage in this situation and get to the heart of the challenge.

At the same time, all too often, Carl will be ignored – he's doing fine, right? But will you keep him fully engaged while you deal with other issues? According to the OVS, people in his group have dramatically different emotional needs. Alignment is an important predictor of performance for people in Carl's group. So to leverage his strength, an emotionally intelligent leader will recognize that need. S/he will help him remain connected to the vital mission of the organization. Again, the KCG process will facilitate this; hypothetically:

Know Yourself: You are anxious about all the balls in the air, and relieved that at least Carl is taking care of business. In the organization, the pattern is, "When someone is effective, give him more," so Carl is getting a lot of work on his plate. Your own pattern is, "When I'm stressed, buckle down and fight," so you're totally focused on the long list on your desk.

Choose Yourself: While the organization's pattern has a lot of benefits, you've experienced the costs when good people burn out. Reflecting further, you see your own pattern "conspires" with the organization's pattern, because when the team is under fire, you actually withdraw to your desk. Focusing on the emotions, you realize that you really want to feel invigorated by the challenge, and you want Carl to feel the same, and supported.

Give Yourself: Your empathy helps you see that Carl deeply cares about the mission, and that you're closely aligned in terms of vision and purpose. So you make a point of catching him on the way to a meeting and appreciating the way he's advancing your shared purpose. You let him know that you personally value his vision and welcome his insight into achieving the important work you're doing together.

The organizational climate is made up of relationships. You improve the climate by attending to the Carls and Joans, one at a time. Attending to feelings at an individual level ripples out to shape the climate – the feelings of the organization as a whole.

One of the most powerful tools you've got for influencing others' emotion is your own emotion. Whether conscious or not, people respond to the unspoken emotional messages you're sending. To know what you're sending, self-awareness is key. As the *Harvard Business Review* cautions, "Executives who fail to develop self-awareness risk falling into a deadening routine that threatens their true selves. Indeed, a reluctance to explore your inner landscape not only weakens your own motivation but can also corrode your ability to inspire others." With increased awareness of yourself and others, and new insight into the emotional drivers of organizational climate, you will deal with your people more effectively. The positive feelings will ripple out, creating a healthier, higher-performing climate.

Again, emotional intelligence is not a "silver bullet." There is no simple formula or prescription. Instead, EQ leaders are aware of the emotional subtext, the unique dynamics of every person and situation. They use that awareness to respond in a way that works with and through people to get results. They perceive what's happening with Carl and Joan, and use that data effectively. They're sensitive

Chapter Eight Recap

Key Concept:

The emotional "tone" in the group or organization is called "climate," and climate drives performance. When people feel good about coming to work, they do better work, they work harder, they take better care of customers, and they are more likely to stay on the job.

Related Reading:

Change or Die, **Alan Deutschman**

INSIDE CHANGE, **Joshua Freedman & Massimilano Ghini**

Key Practice:

Put the organization's emotional tone on the management dashboard; keep considering how decisions are affecting emotions, and how emotions are affecting performance.

To quantify it, use a tool like Organizational Vital Signs on a regular basis (and, ideally, integrate it into the company intranet for continuous feedback): www.6seconds.org/tools

to the emotional messages but aren't overwhelmed by them. They use their own emotions to engage their team members and create a context – a climate – where a diverse group of people can do and be their best.

Chapter Eight Notes

1   Some of this chapter appeared in Joshua Freedman and Thomas Wojick, "The Climate For Success" that appeared on HR.com in 2007. The 2010 Vital Signs Model was created by Massimiliano Ghini, and the new version of the assessment was coauthored by me, Ghini, and Lorenzo Fariselli.

2   Fiedeldey van Dijk & Freedman (2004), *Research Report: Climate and Organizational Effectiveness*, Six Seconds

     For more on Vital Signs, see www.6seconds.org/tools

3   See Freedman, J (2007). *A Hope for Change: Alan Deutschman on Change or Die*, Six Seconds (www.6seconds.org) and Deutschman, A (2006). *Change or Die*, Regan Books

Part Three:

Appendices

Appendix One

Measuring EQ:
Putting it to the Test

This book includes a code inside the back cover. That code will let you take the Six Seconds Emotional Intelligence Assessment (called the SEI), a powerful tool that will help you reflect on the eight emotional intelligence competencies I've discussed in the book.

My team developed the Six Seconds Model in 1997 based on 35 years of experience in teaching these skills. Then we tested the model with thousands of people from over 50 countries. We've used it to help people succeed in individual and organizational change, sales, customer service, parenting, education, and in leadership.

After developing a great deal of curriculum around the model, Six Seconds decided to develop an assessment. Primarily we wanted a tool that would help people with their learning and development – an assessment that would assist individuals in putting emotional intelligence into action in their lives and leadership.

Figure A1.1: SEI Measures

Know Yourself (self-awareness)

- o Enhance Emotional Literacy: *accurately identify and appropriately interpret emotions*
- o Recognize Patterns: *recognize reactions and choices*

Choose Yourself (self-management)

- o Apply Consequential Thinking: *evaluate the costs and benefits of choices before acting*
- o Navigate Emotions: *learn from and transform feelings*
- o Increase Optimism: *identify multiple options for changing the future*
- o Engage Intrinsic Motivation: *build internal energy and drive*

Give Yourself (self-direction)

- o Increase Empathy: *respond appropriately to others' feelings*
- o Pursue Noble Goals: *align daily choices with principles and purpose*

The Six Seconds Emotional Intelligence Assessment measures the same eight competencies you've read about in this book. They are summarized above.

We call the tool "SEI" for "Six Seconds Emotional Intelligence" – and because sei is the Italian word for six, and the tool was codeveloped with our team in Italy.

The SEI toolkit includes a range of EQ assessments and reports for work, school, and life. Unlike conventional tests, the SEI tools are not simply a "diagnostic." Instead, the provide a roadmap for positive change.

Why It Matters

In his best-selling 1995 book, *Emotional Intelligence*, Daniel Goleman reported that research shows that conventional measures of intelligence – IQ – only account for 20% of a person's success in life. For example, research on IQ and education shows that high IQ predicts 10 to 25% of grades in college.[1] The percentage will vary depending on how we define success.

Nonetheless, Goleman's assertion begs the question: What accounts for the other 80%? Goleman and others have asserted that at least some of the missing ingredient lies in emotional intelligence.

As discussed in Chapter Three, there are now numerous studies showing the benefits of emotional intelligence. In Six Seconds' research, we've found that higher scores on the SEI assessment are correlated with a range of important outcomes, including:

- Effectiveness
- Influence

- Decision-making
- Relationships
- Health
- Wellness

Leading to greater success, including
- Career progression
- Financial stability
- Sales
- Leadership
- Individual & Organizational Change
- Customer Service
- Organizational Climate
- Profitability

As discussed in Chapter 3, the skills of emotional intelligence have a dramatic impact on performance. Because these are learnable, measurable competencies, the Model and SEI provide an invaluable framework for tapping human capacity and increasing emotional capital.

More About the SEI

Massimiliano "Max" Ghini, MBA, is a Professor of Management at one of the oldest universities in the West, Alma Business School of Bologna, and is Six Seconds' Director of Global Strategy. Psychologist and researcher Lorenzo Fariselli joined Max to begin the research for the assessment. With continuous research and validation by a team spanning five continents, we've released four editions of the tool, and over 100,000 people have taken the assessment in fifteen languages. In addition to being intensely practical and actionable, the tool is grounded in rigorous science.[2]

The SEI is frequently used in learning and development, selection, coaching, change management, as well as in education (we even have a fully developed Youth Version for ages 7-18).

The SEI is the only assessment measuring Six Seconds Model of Emotional Intelligence. As discussed throughout this book, the Model consists of eight core competencies divided into three key pursuits. Developed to help people put the theory of emotional intelligence into action in their leadership and general well-being in life, the three parts are easy to learn and apply.

The instructions for you to take the SEI are inside the back cover. You will receive a Strengths Report which will help you see your three key emotional intelligence strengths and provide recommendations on how to leverage them. You will have the opportunity to purchase a detailed report with extensive development suggestions, including a one-to-one phone debrief with one of our certified consultants.

Our experience is that the assessment helps people reflect on their own competencies, identify strengths to leverage and vulnerabilities to develop. Please take the assessment and let us know how it helps you.

Notes for Appendix One

1   How well does IQ predict grades in college? Studies actually range from about 2% to 30%. Hunter and Hunter conclude that 25% of college grades are predicted by IQ. *Practical Intelligence* author Robert Sternberg says 10% (e.g., see *Why Smart People Can Be So Stupid*, Yale University Press, 2002).

2   See www.6seconds.org/tools/sei/research for more studies

Appendix Two

Father to Father:
Special Advice for Dads

This is a special chapter, a bonus that I've included because this is part of my own Noble Goal. It's about leadership, but it's not about your business. It's intended for fathers, though others are welcome to read it.

In addition to my role as a leader, I am a father. I suspect many of you are. For me, being a father is the real test of my integrity and quality as a human being. It's the work for which all other work was preparation. If I am nothing but a good father, I will count my life a great success — and if I am everything but a good father, I will know I've failed. And, to be a good father, I also believe that I have to be a good leader and a successful person. It requires a profound shift in thinking away from "work versus family" to a "work and family" vision.

Almost a decade ago, in the first edition, I wrote that, "Today we live in a time of controversy, moral chaos, and fear. Children around the world are growing up in danger, in poverty, inundated with superficial messages about money and sex and power, and more isolated from family and community than any previous generation." I'm sorry to say, I suspect the situation is now even worse.

Are you scared about the influences around your children? I am. I know my children are wonderful, strong, smart, and kind individuals. They have a remarkable level of wisdom – they were 4 and 6 years old when I first started this book, and I learn from them every day. And I'm terrified of what they are facing as they grow up.

In addition to the violence and despair we see in the daily headlines, and the horrifying statistics about global poverty and quality of life for over 3/4 of the world's children, here are a few statistics that alarm me: Around 35% of 15-year-olds world-wide regularly drink alcohol;[1] about 1/3 of US teens are "binge drinking" (5 or more alcoholic drinks at once);[2] one in 10 teens is using hard drugs.[3] Around 35% of 15-year-olds world-wide, and over 47% of kids that age in the US, have had sex,[4] and 12% of high-school girls report having been raped at some point in their lives.[5] About 30% of US teens watch 4 or more hours of television per day, and internationally about the same percentage of boys plays 4 or more hours of video games per day.[6]

Meanwhile, worldwide, 52% of teens have difficulty communicating with their fathers.[7] Social pressures are putting young people at risk, and at the same time they are increasingly isolated; and in itself this feeling of disconnection is dangerous.[8]

Recently in Singapore I observed this dynamic at work. I'm eating lunch at my hotel, and a lovely Chinese family is at the next table. Dad, mom, and teenage daughter – she's dressed up for the occasion. For most of the meal the table is fairly quiet, the girl and dad rarely look at each other. Midway through, mom heads off to the washroom and dad walks out to answer his mobile.

Just then, the girl gets her drink delivered. It's a magnificent pink concoction with spears of fruit and shooting jets of smoke from dry ice. She's sitting alone at the table covered in dry-ice smoke, and I just watch her expression fall. She's disconsolate and lonely — clearly she'd envisioned this moment of excitement and the reality was far from her dreams. What a metaphor for today's family.

There is no easy solution. However, there are easy steps to take. We can use the KCG model to make better choices. We can ensure we're teaching our children the lessons we mean to teach – and we can learn from them. One of the most powerful steps has to do with the way we are "present" when we are with our children.

EQ in the Family

I thought I was getting fairly skilled at emotional intelligence. Then I had children. Nothing in my life has been as challenging – or as rewarding. For me, the real challenge is about doing what I mean to do versus reacting based on my patterns. Being my best versus parenting on autopilot.

My kids are **great** at "pushing my buttons." I bet yours are too. Even when I'm working hard to stay calm and collected, they are able to push me up the Reaction Escalator in a heartbeat. Meanwhile, I know that when I overreact to their fighting, whining, or moping, I'm reinforcing a terrible paradigm.

In their defense, I want you to know that these are two absolutely wonderful little people. Most of the time they are brilliant, kind, and joyful, and my head and heart are full of "snapshots" like:

> Five year-old Emma riding her bike next to me saying, "I didn't use to be 'confident' standing up on my bike, but now look," and zooming ahead standing proudly.

> At bedtime, coming into the kids' room to see them both quietly sitting on Emma's bed "making a movie" with their flashlights.

> Six-year-old Max coming home from school and quietly slipping into my office, seeing me on the phone, and resting his head on my shoulder to say hello.

> Twelve-year-old Emma clutching tightly to my arm in fear and excitement and hope as we drive into the gates of her first sleep-away summer camp.

I want to have more of these. In between there are little moments of explosion. I'd like to have less of those!

The big lesson for me is that when I'm reactive, it really has nothing to do with them – it's all about my seeing myself in them or my being afraid I can't teach them. So the Six Seconds Model is invaluable.

I can ask myself questions based on the model – questions about the eight competencies:

> **Know Yourself**: What am I feeling? What patterns am I following?

> **Choose Yourself**: If I feel and think and use optimism, what options are there? What's the insight in these feelings? What do I want to feel and how can I get there? Where do I find the energy to make that change?

> **Give Yourself**: What's really going on with them? How do I want my interactions with them to affect their world and, in turn, the larger community? What do I want to be contributing to the world?

By reflecting in this way, I can make better choices – and I can keep learning and growing as a father and a man.

Work Versus Family?

Most people I know often feel torn between work and family. To be really successful in most jobs requires tremendous time and energy. Most of my clients and my friends say they just don't have time and energy to do their best at work and at home. I can relate – it's a constant challenge in my life.

I don't have this "all figured out," but when she was about eight years old, my daughter told me something that I'd like to hold onto. I was writing an article and asked her, "What's important in our family?" Among other jewels, she mentioned that, "It's important for Daddy to go help people."

What I got from this simple statement is a big reminder that my kids are watching me. How I talk about my work, and how they see me working, teaches them about work, about responsibility to make a positive difference in the world, and about being a man.

What does your son or daughter know about your work? Does s/he know why you do it? How it is contributing to the world?

I suspect that if I am truly linking my work to purpose – if I can see and feel how my work serves my Noble Goal – then I will communicate that to my family. They will come to see that while I work a lot, my work has real meaning. In other words, my work itself is an important lesson for them.

Now, this is not an excuse for being an absent parent. I travel a great deal in my work; I am often gone for one or two weeks out of a month, so it's a real challenge. When

I am gone I endeavor to connect with them (calling and emailing), and when I get back I set aside more time. I will continue to work on this.

Your Best Leadership Training

As I mentioned, the biggest EQ challenges I face are with my family. So I've come to see that my children are my best EQ teachers. I let myself stay open to their needs and issues and hurts and hopes – I let them challenge me. In so doing, I have an incredible opportunity to grow as a person and as a leader.

Just as employees don't do their very best work simply because of a paycheck, my kids don't do their very best simply because I tell them. I have to use my influence to engage their full commitment. This requires my own commitment, and most of all my own listening. I believe that 90% of what I learn about being a good father transfers directly to being a good leader.

I know that in my role as a leader, one of my big EQ challenges is "staying present." I tend to be thinking three steps ahead, I'm often focused on tasks, and it takes intentional effort to pay meaningful attention to the people around me. This same challenge, of course, plays out at home.

Here's an example of how I can observe myself as a "Self-Scientist" and use my EQ. Observations:

*For one human being
to love another;*

*that is perhaps
the most difficult
of our tasks;
the ultimate,
the last test and proof;*

*the work for which
all other work
is but preparation.*

Rainer Maria Rilke

- The kids are fussing or fighting, so I go into my office, shut the door, and get on the computer.

- I ask my daughter to talk to me about her day, she says, "Fine, I don't want to talk about it," so I go into my office, shut the door, and get on the computer.

- It's near dinner time, my wife is trying to get supper on the table, the kids are "helping," there are toys everywhere, I'm overwhelmed, so I go into my office... you get the idea.

While it's easy for me to justify this behavior to myself, I also recognize there are tremendous costs. I lose intimacy and influence, I don't support my wife and partner, and I teach my kids to follow this same pattern. Ouch!

Applying the Six Seconds Model:

- **Know Yourself**: I feel overwhelmed. My pattern is that when I feel overwhelmed I retreat.

- **Choose Yourself**: When I apply consequential thinking, I see real costs to this pattern. If I navigate these emotions, I see that beneath these feelings is a fear of not being good enough as a father. Beneath that fear is a commitment to give my children the chance to fully live their potential. When I engage my optimism, I begin to see that my choices as a father can truly change the future.

- **Give Yourself**: If I access my empathy, I can see that the children's exuberance is actually an expression of joy. All the noise and mess is a celebration of life. When I reflect on my Noble Goal, it's easy for me to feel that staying present is essential.

Being Present

In chapter six, Choose Yourself, I shared the metaphor of eating dumplings – how it's possible to eat a dumpling and think about something else – or to actually enjoy the dumpling.

The same is true with time with our children (and our partners). We can take time for the daily few minutes of interaction – or we can **give** time, really investing in those few moments.

When my wife and I decided to have children, it seemed that the very stars changed to new constellations. First Emma, and then Max, became part of the constellation. We chose to bring them into the world and committed to care for them. That care requires food to nourish their bodies, education to nourish their minds, and love to nourish their hearts and spirits.

Every day I see clearly how our attention provides the protective guardrails that give them the opportunity to thrive. In the light of our caring, listening, and watching, they are free to explore all corners of their worlds. While

I am not surprised to see this dynamic, I have been quite unprepared for the reciprocation of that illumination. I am only beginning to see how powerfully their attention shapes us, shapes me.

I can not remember a time someone gave such attention to me; I don't remember ever before feeling this sense that my mere presence matters. I come home from a trip, and my children come running calling, "Daddy, Daddy, Daddy," and I know that whatever else occurs in my life: I matter. Often Max will come into my office just checking if I am there, and quietly say, "Hi Daddy," with a little smile, then go on his way. It is like the touch of some angelic spirit resting just within my heart – a moment of indescribable perfection which I hope to hold each day for eternity.

And, sometimes the scrutiny is overwhelming. I want to "just live" and not pay attention to my words and choices. I don't want to be on a pedestal – no, really it is that I don't want that responsibility. I want the illusion of care-free living, that comfortable falsehood that I need only worry about myself.

Fathers tell me it's one of the most difficult times in their lives when they realize their teen children no longer seem to care about them. Intellectually, they know that underneath their "cool" behavior, the kids still care, but the child's focus shifts over time, the world gets bigger, and while daddies remain special, they move to the periphery. And, children say the same about the moment when they realize their parents are just people.

In the meantime, I am storing up memories of unconditional acceptance. For example, I remember when Max entered the room as a toddle. For those of you who don't have toddlers, picture a little person barely able to reach the doorknob, a child who still sees magical wonder in the act of opening a door. Max peeks in, and I don't see him until I look down. He finds my eyes and smiles in the combined delight of discovery and love.

Emma and Max love the water, so when they were little it was tough to get an uninterrupted shower. One day, Max came into the room, and I expected him to want attention or to make some demand. He just came to keep me company. He played "peek" with the towels, and played a little with the water where it collects on the rim of the shower door. When I was done, he chirped, each syllable enunciated, "Bye Dad-dy" and toddled on his way.

I was struck by the way he gave attention, just being present and engaged. How I felt cared for and significant just by his giving me a few minutes of his interest. What a powerful force it is. Desperately, I hope that as his life gets busier and busier, as he gets caught in all the "shoulds" and wants and conflicting commitments of life, that he is able to maintain this astounding ability to influence another person just by visiting with them.

This ability is an incredible gift – one which each of us has readily available. Each of us can increase caring and commitment just with the power of heart and mind. Free for the giver, precious to the receiver, and it takes no more time than passing meaningless pleasantries. How profoundly it would change our workplaces, our schools, our police stations, our government offices, our interactions in the grocery store, our walks in the park, if for a few moments each day we simply gave one another a gift of undivided attention? If we truly looked at one another and smiled just recognizing the fellow humanity we share?

It leads me to I ask myself about all the time I don't pay attention to Max. About last night when I worked late even though I am on a plane today. About this week when I went for a walk with him, but paid attention to my own thoughts instead of his songs. And, thankfully, I also can think about the times when I've noticed my attention slipping from him and redirected it just to be with him, mind and body, for a few minutes.

Maybe it is all I really have to give as a father, husband, leader, friend – those few moments when I focus on someone else, and they can tell that I see them as important. Maslow said each person is born deserving love and loveable – so maybe when people give us attention, it returns us to that core of caring and value. Because it is true – you matter, and the gift of attention that you give matters to the people around you.

Notes on Appendix Two

1. World Health Organization (WHO) policy report, *Health and Health Behavior Among Young People*, 2000

2. Drinking: The Monitoring the Future Survey (www.monitoringthefuture.org)

3. Drugs: Bachman, Jerald G., Lloyd D. Johnston, and Patrick M. O'Malley. Monitoring the Future: A Continuing Study of American Youth (8th, 10th, and 12th-Grade Surveys), 1976-2003.

4. US Centers for Disease Control, Youth Risk Behavior Survey 2004; World data from World Health Organization (WHO) policy report, *Health and Health Behavior Among Young People*, 2000

5. Rape: Compiled by ChildTrends.org from the US Centers for Disease Control and Prevention. Surveillance Summaries

6. Teen Television: Original analysis by Child Trends of Monitoring the Future Data, 1990-2003. Teen video game playing: World Health Organization (WHO) policy report, *Health and Health Behavior Among Young People*, 2000

7. World Health Organization (WHO) policy report, *Health and Health Behavior Among Young People*, 2000

8. For example, the National Longitudinal Study of Adolescent Health, which tracks 20,000 teens, found "Adolescent girls who are isolated from peers or whose social relationships are troubled are at greater risk for suicidal thoughts than are girls with close relationships to other adolescents." Meanwhile suicide has risen to become the third leading cause of death among adolescents and young adults up to age 24. See Bearman, Peter S, *American Journal of Public Health*, January, 2005.

Appendix Two Recap

Key Concept:

Emotional intelligence can help you be a better parent – and being a parent is a great way to practice emotional intelligence.

Related Reading:

The Father I Mean(t) to Be, Joshua Freedman

Numerous articles are available on our site: www.6seconds.org

Key Practice:

Be Present. Give your children some time each day – when you are with them, be with them. Even a few moments of full attention is valuable to them – and to you.

Appendix Three

Recommended Reading

Border M. (1999), "It's the Manager, Stupid," *Fortune Magazine*, October 25

Boyatzis R. and McKee A. (2005), *Resonant Leadership: Renewing Yourself and Connecting with Others through Mindfulness, Hope and Compassion*, Harvard Business School Press, Cambridge, Mass.

Caruso D.R. and Salovey P. (2004), *The Emotionally Intelligent Manager: How to Develop and Use the Four Key Emotional Skills of Leadership*, Jossey-Bass, San Francisco, CA

Cherniss C. (2003), *The Business Case for Emotional Intelligence*, Consortium for Research on Emotional Intelligence in Organizations

Cooper R. and Sawarf A. (1997), *Executive EQ: Emotional Intelligence in Leadership Organizations*, Putnam, New York

Covey S. (2004), *The 8th Habit: From Effectiveness to Greatness*, Free Press, New York

Damasio A. (1994), *The Feelings of What Happens: Body and Emotion in the Making of Consciousness*, Harcourt Brace, New York

Deutschman, A. (2006). *Change or Die: The Three Keys to Change at Work and Life*, Regan Books, Los Angeles

D'Souza, G. (2012), *EQ from the Inside Out*, Six Seconds, San Francisco, CA

Ekman P. (2005), *Emotions Revealed*, Times Books, New York

Freedman J. *et al* (2002), *Handle With Care: The EQ Learning Journal*, Six Seconds, San Francisco, CA

Freedman J. & Ghini, M. (2010), *INSIDE CHANGE: How To Transform Your Organization with Emotional Intelligence*, Six Seconds, San Francisco, CA

Goleman D. (1995), *Emotional Intelligence: Why It Can Matter More Than IQ*, Bantam Books, NewYork

Goleman D., McKee A. and Boyatzis R. (2002), *Working With Emotional Intelligence*, Bantam Books, New York

Goleman D., McKee A. and Boyatzis R. (2002), *Primal Leadership: Realizing the Power of Emotional Intelligence*, Harvard Business School Press, Cambridge, Mass.

Harvard Business Review (2003), "Breakthrough Ideas for Tomorrow's Business Agenda," April 10, 2007

Harvard Business Review (2004), "Leading by Feel," Jan. 1

Martinuzzi, B. (2009), *The Leader as a Mensch*, Six Seconds, San Francisco, CA

Plutchik R. (2001), "The Nature of Emotions," *American Scientist*, July-August

Schwartz T. (2000), "How Do You Feel?" *Fast Company*, June

Secretan, L. (2003). *Reclaiming Higher Ground: Creating Organizations that Inspire the Soul*, The Secretan Center, Ontario

Seligman M. (1991), *Learned Optimism: How to Change Your Mind and Your Life*, Knopf, New York

Sternberg R.J. *et al.* (2000). *Practical Intelligence: Nature and Origins of Competence in the Everyday World*, Cambridge University Press, New York

This book includes access to take the Six Seconds Emotional Intelligence Assessment (SEI) online and receive a free Strengths Report.

To access your EQ Report:

❶ go online to: http://6sec.org/heart

❷ enter your code: KBS9-STCZ

You will receive your report via email after completing the online assessment. For help, email: help@6seconds.org

 Please note: The code can only be used one time